WHAT WE'VE LEARNED SO FAR

Vol.1

An Owner's Manual for Today's Entrepreneurs

Neil Thornton and Larry Anderson

DEDICATION

Neil
To Andrea, Elizabeth and Anna

Larry
To Linda, Sarah and Andrew

CONTENTS

INTRODUCTION
WHAT WE'VE LEARNED SO FAR

Why did we decide to write a book? A few reasons actually.

First when we decided to partner up and form Trigger Strategies we made a commitment to always share what we have learned from the work we do with some of the best small, medium and large companies in Ontario. We believe this stand is about integrity and a strong commitment to business and economic growth. We have gained valuable experience from the private, public and not-for-profit sectors that commonly share similar concerns and challenges.

Secondly, since we each have worked with hundreds of companies and organizations in the field of consulting we felt we had value, ideas and advice to share. For over 20 years we have been learning and writing from the trenches in business. We see value in theory and principles, yet knew that the application and execution of change and growth is what we are asked for most in business owner groups.

Lastly we thought it would be a cool thing to do. We saw the importance of pulling all our work and resources together, lay them out and get them organized in a way that is easy and clear to access. We get asked often to share our experiences and therefore wanted to create a resource for owners and senior managers to find ideas and answers to their daily challenges.

This is not a typical business book. The chapters are short and each one is designed to give you an idea you can put to work immediately in your business. We know how busy business professionals are, and as fellow business owners, we wanted to take that into consideration.

All of the companies we reference are real and we've often worked with them for a number of years. We have chosen to partner with our clients, becoming part of their culture and supporting them through challenges and successes. We do not believe in short term 'information dumps', but instead having a true stake in their outcomes. We've had the privilege of working with great entrepreneurs, dynamic CEO's, senior managers, corporate teams and business owners. All of them have taught us something valuable.

We hope you enjoy the book and we'd love to hear your feedback. Feel free to contact us directly at neil@triggerstrategies.ca and larry@triggerstrategies.ca to share your ideas, comments or to just chat. We would love to hear about your story.

Thanks for reading we really appreciate it.

SECTION 1: **BUSINESS STRATEGY**

"If you fail to plan, you can plan to fail." Napoleon Hill.

Many of you reading this will recognize this famous quote from the book 'Think and Grow Rich'.

When it comes to strategic planning nothing could be more true. Yet over the years in our work with clients and companies we have found that strategic planning is not the most difficult work for an owner or manager; it is 'strategic doing' or 'execution'. In this chapter, we will pull away the veil on this phenomenon and moving target for so many business leaders. We will share what is working and identify some dangerous trends.

We will talk about setting clear vision, its importance and how the future must be the primary focus of any company in language, actions and shared accountability.

We identify how a lack of urgency, follow up and clear expectations will destroy the best pre-planned strategic goals. We will break down how vision needs to live within an organization, progress is made daily and victories are shared. Visions that hang worthlessly on lobby walls are nothing more than wallpaper.

As an owner, senior manager or executive, you play the most important role; leading by example. You are expected to drive change every day. You must show up with focus and enthusiasm, constantly inspiring your team to raise the bar. If all you do all day is firefight, problem solve and babysit; all you will ever produce is more fires, more problems and more babies!

Your vision will pull everyone into action and act as a catalyst. Your strategy gives people the road map. You are an explorer going where no one has gone before. Enjoy the trip.

1
BUSINESS BY DESIGN, NOT CIRCUMSTANCE

"It is not the strongest nor the fastest of a species that survives; but the ones most adaptable to change."
Charles Darwin

The structure of business is changing. Global competition, demanding customers, and shrinking margins are all impacting how we are able to make money.

Your only competitive advantage is your people.

It has been said that, 'People resist change'. In actuality, "People resist the uncertainty of change that is perceived as forced on them." Our role as business leaders, managers and mentors is to allow people to see the true value of change and how important it really is.
When changes arrive on the scene, we hear such comments as, 'flavour of the month' or 'this too shall pass'. This typical 'right or wrong' paradigm is costing us time and money!

Making money today requires investing time in thinking out execution strategies and understanding the forces of changes, by everyone within an organization. Organizations require aligned, connected and competent people to both understand how the business makes money and how to execute strategies.

A new look at business is allowing everyone a 'stake in the outcome'. This statement may sound radical, but for many of us, this is our only option. Our challenge as leaders is to understand what people are committed to and what is important to them. Are they truly in the game?

Imagine an organization where people are able to act on initiative, and creativity. They are not afraid to make mistakes (we only learn when we make a mistake), and they all have a hand in designing the future.

Two fundamental elements of the business are required. The first is an encompassing 'desired future' that everyone speaks and acts on daily. You find this future in language on the floor, instead of hanging in a lobby.

Here is a test: Listen to conversations in your organization. Do you hear conversations about the past, or about a possible future?

The second key element is a true understanding of the 'existing reality' within the business. This reality comes from the discipline to scrutinize what is really happening both inside and outside the organization. Facing the truth and having everyone speak from this truth is essential. A number of elements that get in the way of this step include, assumptions, hidden agendas, trust, ego and fear. The list is actually much longer than this but you get the idea. Effective business leaders can truly identify stories versus reality.

The tension between the 'desired future' and the 'existing reality' creates an advancing structure versus one of stagnation. The critics and cynics in the stands are left behind.

2
FIVE TOOLS TO HELP YOU DEVELOP YOUR CORPORATE VISION

Most business leaders understand how important an encompassing vision is to the organization; yet in our travels it is one of the biggest challenges faced. Why is this so? It is so easy for people to get caught up in the issues of the day, losing focus on future thinking. We hear distractions and excuses like busy schedules, competing silos and poor leadership skills. Although each of these concerns are quite possibly true, our goal here is to give you some direction that can make a big difference in your efforts.

Here are a few actions you can take, and some traditional pitfalls to avoid.

Before you read further you might consider this initial important question.

Is everyone on your team actually on the same page?
If you answered yes, you are free to read on. If you answered no, please contact us or proceed with caution.

1. Get everyone involved
The typical way of doing a vision: owners go on a retreat, word-smithing, sermon on the mount and waiting for change and hoping people will buy in, doesn't work. Vision and goals need to come from the whole team. The engagement of your people is key. Start developing your vision by first establishing a handful of goals, picturing what the future will look like, and then ask your team for feedback and alignment. Ask people what their goals are, what their commitment is, and what they want to see happening. Rarely, if ever will people support a vision they did not help develop.

2. Let your leaders lead

Select a small group of leaders from every level of your organization. This team will be responsible for gathering the needed information and input from the rest of your people. This group will set goals, establish accountabilities and report back on successes. As an owner get yourself out of the way and allow your team to surprise you with their contribution (but also have a plan for those who do not contribute).

3.Dialogue and Listening

Interview everyone in the company face-to-face. Ask them for their honest thoughts, concerns and enthusiasm. You'll find the feedback to be more real and honest this way. Ensure your interview questions are mindfully crafted to enlist commitment to the company, values and ideas for improving service and market growth.

4. Get your customers involved

Next involve your customers. Their candid feedback is essential for the success of the vision.

We highly recommend running what we call a client focus meeting. (You will see us reference this useful business tool often, and more in-depth in section three.)

Bring in 6-10 of your key customers and ask them three questions:
1.Why did you decide to do business with us?
2.Why do you continue to do business with us?
3.What are three things we can do to improve?

Your role is to listen and take notes. The feedback you will receive is priceless. Don't forget to invite a varied group to this meeting including customers who love you, are indifferent or have even left. Developing a vision without your customer's input is like opening a store without any doors.

5. Language, Actions and Accountability

To ensure all of your hard work is successful, you will need to monitor the culture of the company and progress that is made. The vision comes to life through the language, actions and accountability of every employee.
When you get everyone involved from the beginning they take ownership of the vision and live it. People who feel engaged and recognized for contribution will raise the game and stakes for everyone. Get good at giving recognition, it is an integral part of success here.

Once you have mutually developed your organizational vision, the next step is to ensure it is able to be lived, creating innovation and driving change.

3

DOES YOUR VISION STATEMENT HAVE WHAT IT TAKES?

"Is your Vision and Mission statement something that drives every person in your company or just wallpaper in your lobby?"

In the last chapter we advised you how to develop an organization vision. Here are some ideas to help you drive that vision, that could also include a mission, core values and purpose.

If we asked you, or anyone in your company to recite your Vision, Mission and Core Values what would happen? How would everyone do? This is a fair question when it is so important today to be operating from a powerful future instead of mired in day-to-day reactionary tasks.

In our interactions with business owners, we are asked constantly to help them to develop tools that inspire growth, vision and innovation. One major stumbling block is to get people to picture what could be possible for the future, when most are stuck in daily routines and stress. This is not a new challenge for business, but in today's market it is vitally important to break through if you wish to be relevant.

So what makes for a powerful vision? Perhaps we need to look at our past.

Here is a history lesson.

Please think of who said each of the following statements:

"Every household will own an automobile."
"By the end of the 1960's we will have put a man on the moon."
"Every home will own a personal computer."

These statements from Ford, Kennedy and Gates are just a few examples of visionary declarations that have changed the way we live today. One thing you need to understand is these visions were spoken when most people would have thought it an impossible dream. These leaders had an incredible skill of inspiring a nation into action in the face of intense criticism.

So this begs the question. In your organization, what is your IBM Computer? What is your vision declaration that will inspire large groups into action? I am sure it is not something as boring as exceeding customer expectations, quality statements or providing shareholder value (or is it?).

For your company's vision to have courage and guts, it will require some sweat, some fear, some uncertainty but most importantly a belief that it is possible. We would not expect you to know how to get there; only believe that is can be done if everyone raises their game and motivation.

Here are some proven ideas to get your vision off the wall and into language and action:

1. **KISS it!**
    - The best vision statements are simple, clear, one line declarations that inspire everyone.
    - Forget the 'buzz' words and crap language that does not mean anything. (For some real life examples, contact us to inquire.)
2. **Everyone can recite at any time**
    - The best vision and mission statement, including core values can be recited by anyone in the organization at any time, especially outside of work in public.
    - Take the test today, and let us know how everyone does.
3. **People believe**
    - If every person in your company would not take a punch in the gut for the vision, start again from scratch; you don't have it yet.
    - The organizational vision is what gets people out of bed rushing to work, not zombies waiting for payday.
4. **People are inspired**
    - Dr. Martin Luther King did not say, "I have a dream; I just hope we can get enough people to support us and stop complaining in time for something to happen."

- If people are not rushing up to you to share what they have contributed, your problem might be bigger than lack of vision.

5. **Everyone 'lives' the words**
    - People know and understand the importance of actions that are on behalf of the future.
    - They have skin in the game and will challenge others who are falling behind.
    - Living the vision is not driven by the senior mangers alone. Everyone at any level in the organization owns this.

6. **Everyone reports what they have accomplished**
    - Actions, accomplishments, successes and even failures are shared on a regular basis.
    - This is expected and part of your culture of winning

7. **Become a learning organization**
    - All actions taken, successful or not are recorded and posted on a wall for everyone to see.
    - Learning from action becomes engrained in how you operate as a group.

8. **Not Bullshit, no excuses**
    - People may try desperately to dodge accountability here.
    - Don't give in, and be relentless in your expectations.

9. **Picture it**
    - When communicating with others, if you can't picture or see what they are saying, stop them and ask them to better articulate.
    - Words like 'try', 'busy', 'more' or 'better' are not acceptable. (We have many more deleted business words if you want them.)

10. **Get into action now**
    - The downfall of all visions is inaction.
    - Please set up clear follow up plans, and set people up to report back to the group at the next meeting.

With one recent client we helped drive their vision by setting up small teams of committed people to drive contribution and change. This group was responsible as a change agent and they owned the place. This worked very well for them as people felt included and recognized.

Another client used a booklet that was placed at the workspace of someone every day. At the end of the day that person was to write out how they lived and contributed to the vision for that day. They then passed the book along to someone new. They tripled their business in less than three years.

We have many more proven examples that could work for you. Our biggest piece of advice would be to not drive this alone. You will need the help and cooperation of everyone in your company. Getting them on board is your first and hardest task to begin with

4
THE MOST IMPORTANT CHECKLIST
IN YOUR BUSINESS

Once a vision is developed for your organization, the hard part of driving results and managing strategic goals begins. Here are the five critical elements of execution. Checking off each of these elements will start you on your path to success.

"Have you been frustrated with the rate of change and growth in your business? " You are not alone.

For years now we have watched good companies looking to expand business development, change efficiency processes and drive growth, many of which tell us of pains due to plans dying in the meeting rooms. Lack of execution often leads to finger pointing, silo development and endless frustration felt by everyone.

So why do most change initiatives fail?
From our work we have identified 5 key elements required for growth of any kind in business.

- Clear Goals and Strategic Direction
- A Committed Team, ALL On The Same Page
- Everyone Understands What Is Expected Of Them
- The Proper Resources Are Allocated To Innovation
- A Sense Of Urgency Exists

To drive growth all five of these elements must be in place and working in harmony with each other.

5
ANY BONEHEAD CAN CUT COSTS

This section will be a no-holds-barred rant, nothing less. We are going to write the way we think and talk. Our clients expect this approach and nothing less from us; especially in today's market. Welcome to the conversation. PS. No crybabies, whiners or cynics are allowed to read on.

Right now there are two types of companies in operation. The first company is caught up in cutting costs, budgets and training. They are really thinking of nothing else. They see themselves caught up in recession conversations and worried about their changing markets and customers. The pessimists really have a hold on this group. These companies will be left behind, and we are seeing this right now.

We have chosen to work with the second type of company only. This type of organization is using this challenging economy to re-build their team, develop a new offering and reach their clients faster than their competitors. They plan to be the first out of the blocks when we do turn around. We have personally worked with a good percentage of these successful entrepreneurs who have actually told us they have been preparing for this shift. They can now eliminate the dead wood from their team and attract a new group of business thinkers. These companies realize the importance of a long term focus and setting bigger goals. More time is spent being pro-active versus re-active. (Where are you spending your time?)

You see, any bonehead can cut costs and expenses in tough economic times, and most boneheads do. If your only strategy right now is cutting back, you should get out of business as quick as you can.....because you are not a business pro. If you are only doing what your competitors are doing you will not stand out. Does this shake you up? We hope so, as this might be a real wake up for some of you.

Cutting costs is only one strategic initiative. Although it is important to watch cash flow, there are many other things you can be doing right now to strengthen your offering and service to your customers. We would like to offer you a handful of these strategies.

Strategy #1:
Have a true mastermind that will challenge your perceptions and assumptions about your business. Get some real objective outside advice. The 'mastermind' concept comes from the classic book, "Think and Grow Rich", by Napoleon Hill. A true mastermind is a group of business people who you not only trust but keep you accountable by beating the @#%! out of you. This group should challenge you and hold you responsible to grow personally and professionally, it keeps you focused and on track to grow. Who is in your Mastermind Group?

Strategy #2:
Keep engaging and developing your best staff and leaders. If you are not developing yourself and your top performers you will not survive. Spend time with the real contributors, and no time trying to fix people who are not in the game. The top people really understand what is required of them in the growth of the business and act like partners and stakeholders. They expect learning opportunities and want to continue to grow skills and acumen. If done correctly, this is called an investment, not a budget item.

Strategy #3:
Don't lose touch with reality. The way you see the world is rarely how the world really is. Get in a situation where someone can challenge the very assumptions and thought patterns you are making right now. Who is holding up the mirror to you and your thinking right now?

Strategy #4:
Have a clear set of goals and strategies. Keep it simple and everyone sees their role in contributing. People are accountable for producing business results. A sense of urgency exists. (Your #1 goal as a leader is to get people into action.) Vague theories and concepts are left out in the parking lot. Go back to your vision and strategy and ask yourself and others how clear it really is? Does everyone see success the way you do?

Strategy #5:
Contact your key customers today and improve the relationship.
Develop a new offering, provide time or cost saving value, or create a new innovation that will allow your customers to know you are thinking about their business (not yours). Re-connect with your key relationships. See your business they way they see it. Find out how their motivation to work with you is changing. Are your referrals increasing or decreasing? If you are not engaging them by solving their issues, someone else will, typically a flexible and fast moving competitor.

6
WAITING IS NOT A GROWTH STRATEGY

We speak with dozens of business owners and CEO's every month and many of them tell us that sales are slow or declining. So when we ask, "what are you doing about it", we almost always get this answer:

"We're waiting to see if things improve".

Are you kidding us?

It's like they think that the market will miraculously change, their competitors will go out of business and their customers will remember them all of the sudden and just start buying.

That's not how it works.

We run into a lot of companies that have laid out their strategic plans, and somehow they end up in a file drawer, while growth and sales (might as well add in the team members too) sit stagnant.

If your sales are declining it's almost always one of these three reasons:

You are not known by your prospects – a lack of trust – they don't know you because you're not in front of them enough

You are not providing enough value – you're competing primarily on price which means you are viewed as a me-too company or just another vendor

You're not understood by your market – your messaging is all about you and doesn't give a compelling reason to be noticed

Success in sales has a formula: Knowledge + Skill + Action = Results. Nowhere in that formula do you see "wait for things to improve".

Now we know that taking action can be nerve racking. What happens if you take the wrong action? What happens if you make the wrong decisions? But the bigger fear should be what will happen if I don't take action?

We'll tell you the same thing we tell every business owner, CEO and senior manager; don't wait for perfect action, start today taking positive action. You don't need to do everything at once, but you can start with some positive steps like:

Find out who your best customers are and go visit them.
Thank customers for their business and ask for a referral.
Have your business mystery shopped and make improvements to the customer experience.

There will never be the perfect time to make changes. Staff vacations, you hire or fire staff, you get a new competitor, you get new technology or it's year-end. None of that matters; sales growth happens when you take action, and nothing is as important as growing sales.

So what action are you going to take today?

7

HELP...MY TIRES ARE WORN OUT!

"If your car was out of alignment, you would fix it, not just pull on the steering wheel. The same is true for the people in your business and your management team."

When your car is out of alignment there is nothing wrong with the tires (aka your people). The real issue is greater in nature and has developed over a long period of time in the overall mechanics of your car (aka your company).

This is an interesting concept. When your team underperforms this is always the result of misalignment to corporate goals, changing customer situations, vision and expectations. We constantly hear management comments about people's lack of commitment or inability to do their jobs, sometimes even referred to as incompetence. Although there may be a knowledge or execution issue, the root cause is usually tied to clear expectations and accountability.

Getting your team aligned takes much more than yearly retreats or agenda driven quarterly meetings talking solely about to-do lists and operations.

We have facilitated hundreds of meetings where the best conversations happen in the hall after the meeting, or worse yet the team is less aligned to corporate goals afterwards. Most owners or senior managers are not trained to properly get people aligned, so let's try to help. .

Getting your management team truly aligned takes constant check ups, testing, measuring and continuous adjustments....just like the alignment and maintenance of your car.

In a recent management alignment meeting we used the following formula to get everyone working from the same goals and vision. The attendees included the owners, senior managers, working family members and employees. Everyone had an opportunity to write answers to the following questions, then share them with the full group. The context of these questions is more creative and honest in nature, versus traditional problem solving. The key component was the 'group sharing' element, which created a more honest and impactful result.

- **What are the strengths of this team? What do we do well?**
- **As it relates to the business, what is important to you? What do you value?**
- **What are some of the changes you are seeing in our market and our customers?**
- **Do you feel we are changing at the same pace? Yes/No Why?**
- **What are some of the challenges you are facing?**
- **What can we do to better communicate internally and with each other?**
- **What can we do to better communicate externally with our customers? (and vendors)**
- **What changes in the business do you feel will make us more effective and competitive?**
- **What business development opportunities do you see for your department? For the company as a whole?**
- **Do you have a clear business plan to grow your skill sets, your department, and team?**
- **What are your top 3 priorities over the next 2 months?**
- **Do you feel you understand what is expected of you in measuring performance?**
- **What help or resources do you need to better manage?**

Of course, there are many variations of these types of questions that you can use, but the format is designed to share clear goals, strengthen the team, align people to the business mandates and offer help.

As an owner, you will need to be one of the valued participants in this meeting. Please watch out for the classic meeting killers including, hidden agendas, personal conflicts, poor listening and just too much history and baggage. If you really want to drive change, an outside non-partisan facilitator with guts to challenge stories and hidden conflicts may be required to get you to the next level.

You can't fix your car without looking under the hood and knowing what to look for. The same is true with your company.

If you are planning an alignment meeting like this and would like some help, just let us know. Our commitment is to help you drive results, innovation and business development.

8
WAIT A MINUTE…BEFORE YOU HEAD OFF TO YOUR CORPORATE RETREAT

Recently, we received a call from a client looking for some help. He and his management team were preparing to head off for a two day retreat to develop a strategic plan and goals for the organization heading into the new year. He asked us to work with his group of 16 managers to help them prepare ahead of time for the retreat.

As with most owners, he was both excited and nervous about how his investment would provide a return back to the company. He was concerned that what was accomplished and planned on the retreat would not translate back to the organization the following week through action, accountability and measured progress.   Sound familiar? Has this concern ever crossed your path?

The team itself is professional, dedicated, and coming off a record year of sales. All of them expressed how busy they were and found it difficult to spend the time and energy required on this type of planning. They all agreed on the importance of heading into the weekend refreshed, open for growth and prepared to contribute. They were going to require new levels of thinking, contribution and action to ensure their strategic initiatives were going to be carried forward. The owner was worried he would be left with the bulk of the execution while his team reverted back to the same old grind.

I am sure you will agree we all face this same scenario. We head off to strategic retreats, only to have people return back to old habits and agendas that eliminate the best of intentions.

It is our commitment to share with you some 'hands on' tools to help you grow your business. Here is how we handled the meeting.

We asked each manager to articulate a verbal response to each of the following questions:

1. What is your commitment to this group?
2. What will you contribute specifically over the next two days together?
3. How will you choose to be different in thinking and actions?
4. How will you measure committed action and progress the following week?

Your coaching notes for each question:
*   Never assume you know the commitments of your team members. When you assume, you will likely be wrong.
*   Have the group make strong requests of each other.
*   If they remain the same in thinking and speaking, then little will change in the business.
*   Have each person make specific declarations and put something on the line.
*   Remember all conversations are documented for follow up.

As with any group, a number of people responded with vague, weak language. Responses included such things as:

"I hope to help in any way I can."
"I will try to do my best to...."
"I will be a better...."

Through language coaching, we worked with each person to articulate clear measureable goals and remove weak language that included words such as more, better, try and hope. Most of us have been trained in technical knowledge, but few in the use of clear, specific language and communications.

The group left this meeting engaged, energized and excited about the retreat. They all felt they had ownership in the company's success, and agreed upon what was expected of them and the team as a whole. They were already beginning to speak in clear distinct language that included strong requests of each other.

The following Monday, the owner called us with great news. He told us that due to the pre-retreat meeting, his team contributed and worked together like never before. People felt comfortable to make bold stands and commitments with each other. They were able to address real issues and speak the truth. "It was like a new team, with new language." the owner explained, "A new level of respect and trust was evident."

We are proud to share what this progressive team accomplished together. Through some supportive coaching, they were able to strengthen the team and produce some new results together.

9
TWO REASONS ANYTHING FAILS

Ann is sitting in front of her computer screen, searching. Not for a cool new web site, or the latest edition of her favourite blog.

She's searching for answers.

She can't figure out why sales haven't improved. She can't figure out why her staff seems so indifferent. She's searching for answers.

What she doesn't know is that there are only two possible answers. Yes only two.

We'll get to those in a minute.

Ann is not unlike most small business owners. As she looks through her budget and marketing plan she's having a hard time understanding why it's not working. She's increased her budget. She's expanded her geographic sales area. She has fortified her pricing. She's working hard, but the results just aren't there.

So why isn't it working? Here is the solution a great friend of our taught us a long time ago.

It is either DK or DE. DK = Deficiency of Knowledge DE = Deficiency of Execution That's it. There are no other reasons for failure.

We've talked with many, many business owners that have said to us "but money or lack of a marketing budget is why I failed". Wrong. They failed either because they didn't know how much money it would take to do the job properly (DK), or they spent it incorrectly (DE). When you look at your business, and study the areas that are underperforming or causing you stress and frustration, break it down to these two elements, and we promise you will uncover the real problem.

Customer service and indifferent employees are a constant area of frustration for many entrepreneurs. Look at your staff, is it a DK problem: They don't know what to do, or is it a DE problem, they know what to do, but aren't doing it, or willing to do it.

If the problem is a DK problem (lack of knowledge) determine if you or your team have the ability to solve the problem. Remember, the thinking that got you this far may not be enough to solve your problem. Don't be afraid to look outside for help. Friends, other entrepreneurs, customers and consultants can be a great resource to help you.

If you and your team know what to do, then the problem is DE (not doing what needs to be done). Leading by example and reinforcing the behavior you want is the key to success. Changing behavior takes time. It can't be fixed in one training session, so plan on implementing a consistent training program.

With all things being equal the simplest solution is usually the correct one. Look closely at any business problem you're having at this moment in time, it will come down to DK or DE. How you solve it is up to you. If you need some help we are just an email or call away.

10
DON'T I KNOW YOU?

We were at a client's last week meeting with his entire team – a group of about 15 employees. We asked them the following questions:

- Do you know who the top 20% of your customers are?
- Would you know the last time they came in?
- Do you know the average purchase of your top customers per visit?
- Do you know how much you get of the total dollars your top customer spends on your category?
- Do you know what a customer is worth?
- Do you know what a top 20% customer is worth?
- Do you know how many times per year your top customers buy from you?
- When was the last time you connected with your top customers?

Every employee answered all of these questions the same – including the owner:

I DON'T KNOW.

We can't say it surprised us. But it does alarm us and if you can't answer these questions about your business you should be very frightened as well. As business owners we spend most of our time and marketing budget trying to find and win over new customers. It's a very expensive activity. But once we find these elusive customers and win them over we have to keep them.

Here's another question for you – Do you think it's easier to sell to someone who knows you vs. someone who doesn't?

Let's take a closer look at your existing customers:

- You know who they are (if you're recording their information).
- They like you (if you've provided value).
- It costs less to communicate with them (if you have their correct contact information including email or social media).

Now let's look at your new customers:
- You don't know them (you have to try to find them in a sea of people who aren't interested in buying from you).
- They're bombarded with 5000 messages a day competing for their attention (by the way we block out 99% of those messages).
- If they do buy what you sell, they're already buying from someone else whom they know and like.

So here is your game plan.
- If you're not already doing this, start collecting customer data today.
- If you have been collecting customer data, make sure it's accurate.
- Learn about your customers – when they like to buy, how often, average purchase, main problems they need solved.
- Identify your top 20% - here is a hint, if you lost one of these customers you would need 10 regular customers to replace them.
- Start communicating with them on a regular business – not about you – don't sell – give them value.

11
WHICH ONE ARE YOU MISSING?

Insert stunned looks. That's usually what we get when we ask a business owner or CEO to specifically explain how they are going to grow sales.

Now you wouldn't think that would be the case. These people typically are very smart and run successful companies with good people working for them, but when we ask about sales, they get uncomfortable and unsure of themselves. We have witnessed this scenario often over the past few years.

We primarily work with companies that have between 15 – 300 employees and sales planning for them is a little like fortune telling. It's mostly guessing and wishing and unfortunately a lot of smoke and mirrors. Now we're sure you're going to tell us that you're different, but stay with us for a second.

While there will never be a perfect way to forecast what your sales will be for the next year, there are five strategies that if you have them in place will give you a much better chance.

Current customers

There is a term used in marketing called "Share of Customer". This refers to how much of a customer's business you are getting. If they normally spend $100 a year on what you sell and they spend $50 with you, you are getting a 50% share of customer.

Many companies leave dollars on the table because they don't properly educate their customers on everything they do or they don't stay in contact with customers and a hungry competitor steps in.

Remember, it is much easier to sell to someone who already knows you, likes you and has purchased from you than to try to find a brand new customer.

Past Customers

We have seen this happen at least 100 times over our 20-year careers. We'll say to our client – "Please have your sales team call all of your customers that haven't purchased from you for at least 1-2 years over the next two weeks". Wham! They get new orders and rekindle old relationships. We've seen it produce a 20% bump in sales for some firms.

Push prospects

Push tactics include your advertising, direct mail and email campaigns. These are the leads that come in through your marketing efforts. The good news is that the prospects that make contact usually have an immediate need for your services. The bad news is that they're usually looking at other options as well and price becomes a big factor.

But push tactics are important to help establish your brand position in the market and to keep you "top-of-mind" with prospects that need what you sell.

Pull prospects

Pull tactics include social media, your website and content marketing. Your goal here should be to establish yourself as an expert resource. The key is to develop information that your prospects will find valuable and want to consume via different media like text, web, video and audio and share it via social media and direct to their colleagues, friends and customers.

This process can be time consuming and take some time to build momentum, but the relationships and connects you make using these tactics lead to larger and more profitable customers.

Direct Prospects

This usually involves an outside sales team where you target specific prospects that you would like to work with. This is typically combined with pull tactics as well as direct contact.

The main goal of a direct contact campaign is not to "sell"; rather your goal is to qualify.

When you execute a direct campaign, it should consist of a series of "touches" or contacts over a period of time. Your touches can include letters, articles, videos, phone calls, gifts, referrals, reports and links to relevant information. Just remember to keep everything focused on the prospect and **DO NOT SELL**. Give away your insights and expertise. Show them you understand their business and that you have helped solve problems they may have.

Remember 'no' is not forever. If you have done your research on the prospect and you know you can help them, keep in front of them. Just because they don't need you today, doesn't mean they won't need you tomorrow.

So as you can see to have sales success for your business it's important to have a strategy for all five of these elements

Many of the firms we work with initially only focused on one or two of these strategies and wondered why their sales were flat or declining.

As one of our clients said to us just recently "the getting is more important than the doing". While it's critical to deliver a superior customer experience it can't happen if you don't first get the client.

12
WHAT DO YOU WANT TO BE KNOWN FOR?

No matter what we do in business, we're going to be compared to someone else. When a customer is in the market for what you sell, they're going to look at your competitors and compare you.

So the questions are: What do you want them to think about you? What do you want to be known for?

The greatest challenge for you is, what happens if what you want to be known for is not what you ARE known for? What do you do then?

Customers are won and lost based on how they perceive your value. Perception is king; what the customer thinks and believes is what matters.

If you want to be the highest quality, but one of your competitors has been saying it and proving it longer than you, they will own that position in the customers mind. You will always be second.

So what it comes down to is, what **can** you be known for? Because the last thing you want to be is a "me-too" company. It's also about being able to deliver on your promise.

So how do you do this?

1. Take a look at your company – what are your true capabilities. To be known for something, you must be able to prove it and have the credentials.

2. Look at your competitors – who owns what in the market place? What are they known for and how do they deliver on their promises?

3. Talk to your customers and determine what is most important to them. Don't do a formal survey, rather have conversations with them and watch how they interact with your staff.

4. Talk to your front line employees. They're the ones that talk to your customers everyday. Learn what customers are saying and what your employees think.

5. What is your vision for your company? What do you want to achieve? When you close your eyes and look ahead 1-3 years what do you see?

These five steps will help you gather the information you need to start to see a clear picture of where you are now and what you can be.

But the most important thing to remember is that once you have determined what you want to be you have to live it everyday in everything you do. There are no shortcuts. You need to be real, authentic and transparent or your customers will see right through it.

13
THE ENGAGEMENT STRATEGY

Ok; you've cut as many overhead costs as you possibly can to remain competitive. You are running as lean as possible, and you have fewer people doing a larger share of the work. You have cut as many budgets as possible, including training. (Oops, that one may come back to haunt you.) Stress is high and it is getting more difficult to motivate people and stay focused. You have more on your plate, and it seems to increase daily.

With all this change the competition continues to gain momentum, and your market share is becoming more difficult to capture and maintain. Your customers are demanding more and your offering is being stretched to the limit.

Does this sound familiar? For many organizations today, this is a brutal reality we face.

So what is next? Where do we go from here?

Quite possibly the only competitive advantage remaining is your people. Actually, this was always your largest advantage in the marketplace. The battle for talent and retaining skilled people remains a top business issue, yet a recent Canadian business survey identified that 83% of people working today are not engaged in their company. 83 PERCENT!!!!

In other words only 17% of people working today consider themselves as real contributors to the organization and truly involved in the growth and strategy of the company. This number can change and there are some unique companies doing just that. These companies are choosing to become an employer of choice.

8.5 Ideas to engage people in your organization.

1. Consider people as entrepreneurs instead of employees. Give them a stake in the outcome. Clarify to them what is really happening in the marketplace.

2. Identify and communicate success.
Use 'person centered feedback' and back it up with real examples. Please remember the number one human need in business: "Recognition of a job well done".

3. Involve all levels of staff in strategic and organizational planning. Quite often the best ideas are generated on the shop floor, back office or amongst front line workers. Truly listen to what they have to say.

4. Get the organizational vision off the wall in the lobby and into daily conversations. This one may be tough and you may need some help. The payoff is tremendous when everyone is talking about a dynamic future. Those who choose to remain in the past, instead of creating a new future are left behind.

5. Abolish yearly performance appraisals. Replace with monthly feedback sessions focused on future action and accountability. For additional guidance you will find in this book *The Paper Lion, Abolishing Traditional Performance Appraisals*.

6. Structure meetings that create accountability and capture learning.
Balance management skills with mentoring and coaching sessions. Allow people to see their potential and strengths. Coach everyone for performance improvement.

7. Know that all people are committed. Get genuine commitment and alignment will follow. Never question someone's commitment; find out what it is.

8. Never openly criticize, condemn or complain. *"Any fool can criticize, condemn and complain as most fools do." Dale Carnegie.*

8.5. Communicate, communicate and communicate.

These skills are not easy. Yes, developing and engaging people is a job that never ends, but the payoff of having committed people all contributing to the growth of the business (versus slowing it down) is amazing to see in action. The soft side of business has now become the hardest side of business.

"If your people are not having a positive impact, or contributing to the strategy of the company; they are simply liabilities."

14
ARE YOU GETTING BETTER?

Warning: This article may be offensive or difficult to read if you are a victim, feeling out of control, or cowering in the corner waiting for the economy to get better.

"Your business will get better when your people get better. Your people will get better right after their manager gets better." Many of you may recognize this quote if you have ever worked with us. It has certainly elicited some honest feedback from our clients and has shaken a few people into action. As business consultants, it is our stand and choice to constantly influence people to improve, regardless of outside factors.

In Ontario, cutbacks and layoffs are at an all time high. Economic uncertainty surely has its share of attention in the media. For many of the progressive companies we work with, current strategic conversations are centered on keeping focused, executing long term business goals, and re-building the best teams and people to succeed. These teams include people willing to contribute at higher levels of commitments and skill sets. This will include you.

This is where you come in. Right now there is a conversation going on about you in your organization and the impact you are having. If you are a small business owner this conversation may be taking place with your customers. Everyone is included here. From years of experience working with companies, we have seen too many people standing on the sidelines unaware of these conversations. This example showed up for us in a recent episode of Survivor, when a candidate who was voted out of his tribe explained, "It was when I became comfortable and confident, that I was blindsided by my team." Can this 'reality show' example carry over to business? You bet.

Let's consider this article a strong call to action. Are you up for a challenge? Here are a few questions for you:

1. In the last year, what specifically have you done to improve yourself and your skills? No vague theories please just hard evidence.

2. What courses have you taken, on your own accord, to improve your value to the company?

3. What books have you read in the past year that you can transfer back to your team? Right now, many of our clients have us asking these questions in most performance conversations. There are many more questions, but we are sure you get the point.

Recently we were asked to interview two candidates for the same senior management position. The first candidate (only 2 years with the firm) was energetic, enthusiastic about learning and eager to improve her skills. She was well respected by her colleagues and constantly challenged others to improve as well. In the interview, she produced a number of course certificates, many of which were sourced through her own personal resources. The second candidate was a 20 year veteran, confident that he would be awarded the position due solely on his seniority. This candidate did not believe in self improvement and felt it was the company's job to make him better. (Whatever that meant?) When the decision came to offer the job to the first candidate, we were given the task of bearing the bad news to the second. Of course, when the seniority card was pulled, our response to him was quick and to the point. "You have only worked here one year, twenty times!"

So what does this have to do with you? We challenge you to be the person that is being considered part of the new team, ready to build your company in the new global economy that is coming at us. Please take your contribution and improvement seriously. Please do not be the one left behind wondering what happened when you got voted out.

"If you are not having a positive impact on the people around you and the company's bottom line, you are nothing more than a liability."

15
MOMENTS OF TRUTH

How many customers did you lose today? You may be surprised. Every time a customer or potential customer comes in contact with some aspect of your business, they form an opinion or a perception of what your business is. These are called Moments of Truth.

This concept was first developed by Jan Carlzon former CEO of Scandinavian Airlines.

Every time a customer makes a purchase, there may be up to 30 Moments of Truth in that single transaction. Each time a customer has interaction with your business, it's an opportunity to both build loyalty and win the customer back for another sale, or to lose the customer, possibly forever.

Perception is reality. If your customer sees the outside of your office and it looks dirty or unsafe, that forms their opinion. If your web site is out of date or you don't have one, that also forms an opinion. You've spent a lot of time, money and energy creating this business of yours. You've dreamt of how it would look, you've sweated over your location and store layout and you are very protective of everything about it.

Guess what; you may still be giving customers the wrong idea about what your business is all about.

Customers interact with your business all the time without interacting directly with you. Do you have a web site? Do you advertise? Do you have staff? Do customers use the products and services they purchased from you? Don't leave it up to chance. Walk through your business with a customer's eyes. See things from their point of view. Look at every touch point from your web site and advertising to your store layout, merchandise and staff.

Are you delivering a consistent message to customers, no matter who the customer is talking to?

Are you delivering consistent service every time the customer shops with you?

Are you giving customers a reason to come back or look elsewhere?

16
MISTAKES VS. FAILURE

Some of the greatest things we've learned in our life came right after we fell flat on our face. Mistakes are wonderful learning opportunities, painful, but opportunities to learn just the same.

It was 1996 and Larry was four years out of college still trying to figure out his career and about to embark on a journey that would be one of worst and one of the greatest lessons of his life.

Larry always had a natural ability to sell, and because of that he was getting a reputation in his job with a newspaper company as a sales problem solver.

This caught the attention of a couple of self-made publishers and before he knew it he became a co-owner in a newspaper and magazine company.

We won't bore you with all of the gory details, but we will share two stories with you.

Ego can kill you

Larry entered into this new business and partnership not knowing anything about business. All he knew (and he didn't even know this he just thought he did) was sales and marketing. So when he was asked to be part of it, his ego got way too inflated and he went in eyes shut and full of bravado. Big mistake.

The biggest lesson Larry learned was that what you don't know, you don't know can really hurt you. He was young and thought he knew a lot or if he didn't that he would out work everyone. Wrong, you need to know your stuff and surround yourself with people who are smarter and better than you are.

Larry didn't listen to the voices of reason around him (mostly his wife) and he just kept going on blind faith that this doomed enterprise would someday turnaround and be profitable.

It didn't and Larry learned to never let his ego get the better of him again.

Know your partners

Partnerships can be great (like the one we have now) or terrible like the one we're going to tell you about.

Larry went into partnership with three guys that he didn't know very well at all. No background with them. Because they fed his ego, he just went in.

We're not going to drag them through the mud here because Larry alone is responsible for what happens to him; rather we're just going to explain that a partnership is built on two things – trust and accountability.

Larry didn't know these guys so he had no experiences with them, nothing to base the relationship on, so it was just faith. He also didn't really know their strengths, so because he was the new guy and the junior partner he didn't feel he had the right to question them.

We've seen a lot of small business people go into partnership with someone mostly because they were afraid to go out on their own, or they are following a blind hunch. This is the wrong thing to do.

Lesson: only have a partner if you really need one. That person is someone you trust completely, you can rely on when things get tough and that they will do what they say they will do. They should also have a completely different set of skills than you. And most important, they will call you on your shit.

Now why did we share all of this with you? Two reasons:

If we can save one small business owner the grief Larry went through, we're more than happy to do it

Secondly and most importantly we want you to understand the difference between mistakes and failures. To some people this part of Larry's life was a huge failure, but to him it was a huge mistake that he learned valuable and multiple lessons from.

A mistake only turns into a failure when you make that mistake repeatedly and don't learn from it. Mistakes are good; it means you're trying something new. It means you're pushing yourself.

So we encourage you to make mistakes, lots of them. Keep pushing yourself and going after new goals, just pay attention to what's happening, put your ego aside and learn.

17
HOW TO CUT YOUR MEETING TIMES IN HALF

As a business owner or manager, we are sure you will agree the number of meeting commitments can seem daunting and a huge drain on your most important daily resource…time.

It is frustrating to watch countless people walk into meetings looking like the cast of The Living Dead. It is even worse to observe the best dialogue happening in the hallway, after the meeting.

Are meetings important? You bet they are. So why are they so despised by productive and active people on your team? The answer is simple…your meetings probably suck.

We have been involved in meetings with hundreds of companies and teams. We have seen what works and what does not. We have been the unfortunate facilitators of bad meetings and we have ourselves walked out of boardrooms banging our heads against the projector.

We have learned a lot along the way and by studying great meeting leaders in action our game has improved.

We would like to share with you some of the recommendations we share with our clients. We hope you can apply some or all of these with your team.

- **Have a written agenda.** The agenda should be sent out ahead of time to the meeting participants. They will have an idea of what is expected of them and they can adjust the format if required.

- **Meeting time is for reporting not always assigning.** When your group is together they should be reporting back on commitments and accomplishments that have been pre-assigned. This keeps the group engaged, moving forward and contributing.

- **Assign only at the end.** Get a quick consensus of what needs to happen and agreement at the end of the meeting. This sets the stage for the next meeting and assignments are sent out formally afterwards.

- **Problem solve when required.** Many meetings are fraught with problem solving dialogue and endless analysis, often centered on a few individuals, and leaving out others. If a major problem or issue exists, and was not an agenda item, have a separate focus group create solutions outside the meeting. They can bring solutions back to the group. If all you do in meetings is problem solve, you will only ever create more problems.

- **Huddle up team.** Great companies today are holding 'standing meetings' where the boardroom is replaced with the shop or office floor. People are energized on their feet and time is respected. Everyone has a few moments to comment and respond. The meeting ends quickly and people get back to work.

- **Stop watch and time.** Give everyone a pre-determined amount of time to communicate with the group. Use a stop watch and alert people of time remaining. Call out 'time' and move on. This practice helps develop discipline and will eliminate one person from stealing meeting time with verbal diarrhea.

- **Meeting costs are understood.** If you have 10 people in a meeting with an hourly expense of $90 per hour, taking into consideration all other financial overheads, everyone needs to understand what meetings cost.

- **No one leaves without a commitment.** The biggest killer of any meeting is when everyone talks and talks, but nothing ever gets accomplished. No wonder apathy exists. After every meeting, please develop a document outlining commitments, action steps and accountabilities. The next meeting will open with people reporting back on what they have completed.

- **Get good at speaking.** Your agenda may be the best ever written, but if you can not engage people and drive them forward, please NEVER lead another meeting. Ultimately, people are looking to be inspired into action. This does not mean you have to become a motivational speaker, but your style MUST create a motivating environment for people to rush out of room to get into action. How good are you at this? How will you get better?

- **Have a smartphone basket at hand.** Ever notice Shelly at the end of the table looking down to her lap? She is not looking at her shoes. In all meetings, cell phones and devices are turned OFF or deposited in the basket.

- **Start and finish on time.** Meetings start at the set time, no excuses no late arrivals unless the full group is advised and apologized to. As well, meetings end on time. If you want people to respect you and arrive on time, please return the commitment to finish on time.

- **Stop pontificating.** We have all been there. The president stands and starts her dissertation about the state of the world. "When will this blow hard shut up, please shoot me now," can be heard whispered around the table.

Have you ever found yourself violating any one of these? We certainly have. So what works for you? What would you add to this list? Please let us know, we will update it and reference you with your permission.

18
COACHING FOR A CHANGE

"You can not solve a problem with the same mind that created it."
Albert Einstein

In business today, we would translate this famous quote to read, *"You can not grow your results with the same mind set, habits and thinking that got you to this point. Breakthrough growth is going to take a whole new way of seeing yourself, your team and your customers and creating something that does not exist in the market today."*

We are speaking from experience when we say that most businesses, to succeed today, require an entirely different model and offering than it had just two years ago. The tough part for all of us buried in the operations of our organizations is spending the time and energy required to challenge our traditional habits, operations and even customer offering to hit new levels of performance and results.

As certified consultants and coaches with years of experience, we find ourselves spending the majority of our time 'coaching coaches' to work within their organizations with their teams. These people realize the fact that no one will ever hit stretch goals on their own. The best they can hope for is incremental growth if they choose to stay on the same path. This is no longer good enough in business.

49

Our commitment has always been to get coaching, communications and leadership tools to as many people as we can. While we are not in front of you now, we wanted to give you a coaching conversation module we use with our clients. Please use this tool first with yourself and then use it with your key team members. (Have a trusted colleague walk you through the questions. Remember you can not coach yourself!)

- What is one strategic 'stretch' goal you choose to accomplish in the next 30- 60 days?
- What's missing, that if it were in place, would make all the difference for you?
- What are you willing to invent, that you have yet to invent, that will give you more options?
- Where are you willing to be different, in thinking, behaviors and actions that will allow for better results?
- What assumptions (or ego) must you eliminate that will allow you to hit this breakthrough goal? What must you let go of? (This is a hard question for most people.)
- What strong requests do you need to make of the people around you to receive the support and accountability you need?
- How 'serious' are you about challenging your old ways of operating to hit this new level of performance?
- What is your first step and how do you want to be held accountable. (If a commitment is made follow up MUST exist.)
- Are you open for strong coaching that will allow you to be challenged and hit this breakthrough goal? Are you ready to get yourself out of the way?

In the absence of strong organizational coaching, we see many good people stuck in comfort zones and, over time, become resistant to change. You must know that people do not resist change, but the uncertainty of change. Your role as a coach, and ultimately a leader is to develop a culture that sees change as an opportunity to contribute and grow.

There are many components to the world of coaching and getting help from a certified, experienced coaching professional is highly recommended. In the meantime we hope this article gives you a head start with yourself and your team to compete in the new speed of business.

SECTION TWO: **TRAINING**

Einstein said *"once you stop learning you start dying".*

We know that in today's competitive business world the only true competitive advantage you really have is your people and if you're not investing in them you are falling behind.

In the same manner, if you are part of a team and not constantly building skills, acumen and personal and professional skills, you will quickly become irrelevant.

We have asked countless teams to rise up and agree that markets, customers and their own company is changing; and then ask them to continue standing if they are personally changing 'faster' than the three indicators. It's concerning to observe what typically happens next.

We hear of people who resist change, development or training programs. We label that people resist change. That is not true. In fact, people resist the uncertainty of change that is perceived as forced on them. Interesting perspective.

Everyone is busy today and using this is an excuse to learn new skills and perspective is instant death for your business. Although the training landscape has drastically changed, there are a lot of options to choose from. This 'busy' excuse is no longer allowable.

We have worked with hundreds of business owners and thousands of individuals in the area of training, development and coaching. We have facilitated classroom settings, late night hotel conference rooms and early morning shop talks. We have lead learning programs on job sites, factory floors, boardrooms and coffee shops. We have seen it all. The one constant rule remains. Those who invest in themselves will always rise above the crowd. Those who offer up excuses will fall behind.

Remember as an owner you must never develop training programs to fix people. The best programs are offered to those who choose to request and accept learning as part of their business plans. Goals and objectives are clear.

Don't attempt to turn ducks into eagles. It pisses off the eagles, it pisses off the instructors and it pisses off the ducks too. Start with figuring out who your ducks are and who your eagles are. Focus on your eagles.

So where do you start?

Like you, we are also business professionals, so when we wrote this chapter we wanted to provide thoughts and actions steps you can apply right away to your business. The following pages should give you some clear ideas on how and where to start with your team.......and yourself while you're at it.

19
THE MOST VALUABLE THING YOU CAN DO RIGHT NOW IN YOUR BUSINESS

If you are like most progressive companies, you are looking for ideas to strengthen your team and produce some solid results. You see that your continued success in the next few years will be determined by your people and how they support your strategy and each other.

In the absence of truly understanding and knowing the people you work with, you will each be driven by your own agendas, schedules and priorities. This misalignment can cost you valuable time, resources and productivity. Each person you work with is unique in how they think and consider themselves a contributor to the team. As companies continue to develop an engaged and aligned group, they are seeing the need to develop clear expectations, goals and work habits. Please NEVER assume you know how people operate and what is important to them. When you 'think' you know, you will always be wrong.

We wanted to get this tool to you as part of this book. If you are serious, and we mean SERIOUS about aligning your team, you will need to really understanding what makes your group operate in a cooperative and supportive way. There are no excuses allowed here. Being 'busy' does not count. (Who isn't busy?!) Please have every person on your team complete the following questions......today! This exercise should be the most valuable thing you do all year.

SURVEY: How I Choose To Work and Value My Contribution

- This is how I would describe my work style

- My most effective and productive work environment would look like
- This is how I best communicate with others: (In certain situations.)
- This is how I like to be communicated with
- My most productive time of day is: This is how I best work at this time
- I feel this is how you can help me the most right now
- I wish to contribute in the following ways
- This is how I wish to be held accountable
- Our meetings would be more productive if we
- This is how I like to receive feedback from my colleagues and manager
- This is how I like to be recognized
- This is what is most important to me, as it relates to my career
- What I value most is
- My real strengths would include
- I feel my input matters when I receive the following feedback
- This is how I would describe my character and attitude:
- This is how I choose to better my skills and attitude
- I am most comfortable at work when
- My top 3 professional goals include
- The critical factors (3 main goals) of my work right now are
- This is how I prefer to be taught
- This is how I manage my time
- This is how I like to re-charge and re-focus
- I feel that I am the most creative when
- My next steps in learning new skills include
- This is how I wish to review my performance
- What I see getting in the way of my progress includes
- I prefer to handle stress by
- This is how I tend to handle difficult situations
- This is how I tend to handle difficult conversations
- Our greatest strengths as a company are
- Our customer service makes us distinct because
- Our biggest challenges in the next year will be
- Our clients do business with us because
- What is going to allow us to compete in the future will include:

And finally.....I feel what is expected of me includes: (Please feel free to adjust based on your work environment.)

We think you get the picture here. We have included a good variety of questions that will allow any team to understand its players at a deeper level.

20

PEOPLE ARE EITHER LEARNING OR LEAVING

For years now, we have witnessed good companies consistently develop their team and train them for improved skills, both technical and behavioral. We have also seen companies that have put training and development on the back burner, and are now facing the ramifications and consequences of that decision.

Without development opportunities the brutal reality shows up. People lose the interest, motivation and engagement to contribute. They are literally 'checking out' because they are not growing and learning. It is always disappointing to see people who decide 'to leave the job, but stay on board'. In one instance I overheard a senior manager say to a group of colleagues, '*Twenty five more years and I am out of here.*' Ouch.

There are a number of reasons why companies have cut back on training. The primary one is due to budget restraints. This is the reality for most companies right now, but that is no reason to stop training and development programs. People may say they are not interested in training, but we guarantee they want to contribute more and continue to learn. Your role as a leader is to lead by example, show them the importance of ongoing development, and link it back to the improved business results required to compete today. *The business will get better when its people get better; and people will get better......right after their manager gets better.*

We wanted to give you a tool you can use to help your team develop, and it costs very little. Get them to 'read'. Here is how it works. Whether you have 5 or 25 key leaders, go out and purchase the same number of copies of a classic book. (Audio books work well too.) Have every team member read a chapter or two independently. Then ask them to come together and 'teach' the rest of the team:

1. What they learned.
2. The key concepts that will help the full team.
3. Their commitment and challenge for the rest of the group to apply the idea(s).
4. How progress will be measured.

We have run this exercise on many occasions and the results have always been amazing, whether in a large or small group. What you are doing is setting the expectations of a learning organization and allowing people to share and teach what they gained. This ensures the material 'sticks'.
If you are looking for good books to get started here are some of our favorites:

"The Little Red Book of Selling", Jeffery Gitomer (Sales)
"Good To Great", Jim Collins (Growth & Quality)
"The Art Of Possibility", Ben Zander (Breakthrough Thinking)
"How To Win Friends and Influence People", Dale Carnegie (Human Relations and Communications)
"How To Stop Worrying and Start Living", Dale Carnegie (Stress and Worry)
"Think and Grow Rich", Napoleon Hill (Planning and Vision)
"The One-Life Solution", Dr. Henry Cloud (Balance, Focus, Time Management)
"The 21 Irrefutable Laws of Leadership", John C. Maxwell (Leadership)

Please let us know how this works for you. Success stories are always fun to pass along.

21
HOW TO KNOW YOUR TRAINING PROGRAM IS GOING TO SUCK

Dear business owner. You have realized that training your people to improve skills and performance is essential to growing (or even maintaining) your position in the market. You understand that not training your top performers has resulted in slow (or no) growth, apathy, or even good players leaving your company.

You have sourced out training options; and there are lots to choose from. Before you engage any outside training firm, can we please ask you to consider the following key points of why many outside training and consulting approaches could be a complete waste of time and resources? If you find yourself repeating any of these statements, hold up.

- *"I want to find training that will fix my people."*
- *"Everybody tells me they are too busy to take training."*
- *"I am not involved in the process or design of the program."*
- *"I am not taking part in the training with my team."*
- *"My people did not ask for the training, nor are accountable to improve skills."*
- *"The trainer we hired has not run a business and is not a business person."*
- *"What type of performance guarantee did I get?"*
- *"There is no accountability or follow up."*
- *"We hired a motivational speaker....what now.....?"*
- *"There are too many tips, techniques and theories, not enough practical application."*
- *"I have a binder on my bookshelf....now what?"*
- *"What is the business relevance of the training?"*
- *"How will the training really impact our bottom line of increased sales or efficiency?"*
- *"The trainer went back to the head office far away....now what?"*

What options do you have now?

In our extensive experience, we recommend that as an owner you involve everyone in the development and facilitation of any training. In truth, you know what you need to do; you're just not doing it. All training must be established on behalf of people's commitment to improvement, their understanding of changing markets and having them request training based on aligned expectations.

We have had over a decade of success helping companies design their own programs developed by everyone in the company. This type of program belongs to the organization, and people take ownership in the success of the development. People want to see it succeed because they helped build it. The material is owned by you and able to be replicated easily and taught by everyone. Your key leaders are the facilitators, not someone who blows in and out.

You can bring in outside people to help facilitate and coach, and even bring materials, but they must augment and add to your existing program, not replace it.

Sound good? Drop us a note and we can help you walk through your own program

22
HOUSTON, WE HAVE A COMMUNICATIONS PROBLEM

We work with many business teams and it always blows our mind when we get the whole company in a room and ask, "How many times a year do you meet like this" and we hear "we rarely if ever meet like this".

So it's no surprise when we hear time and again they have a communications problem at their company.

B.S.

They have a perceived communications problem when really it's about expectations.

When we dissect what "communications problem" means, it usually comes down to "I never know what's going on outside of my department", or "I did what they (management) asked me to do, but they're never happy".

One definition of communication is "The imparting or interchange of thoughts, opinions or information by speech, writing or signs".

What's missing from that definition is the word understanding.

When you ask your staff to do something, you have a picture in your mind of what it will look like when completed. So does your staff, but it's not always the same picture.

For example, you give your sales team a list of past customers and you instruct them to call everyone on the list and reconnect. A week later you sit down with your team and ask, how the project went and you hear "I called them but they never called back".

Your expectation wasn't to have your team leave messages, you wanted them to keep calling until they got someone on the other line, while your team thought it meant leave a message. Your team didn't understand your expectations.

90% of the problems we see between people in the companies we work with can be tied back to unknown or misunderstood expectations.

How to align expectations

- Clearly state what the completed task will look like, how it will be measured, what resources are required and when you expect it completed
- Ask your team for input as to how they feel it can be best completed
- Have your team give you a plan (depending on the size of the project it can be a paragraph in an email or a 2 page document) as to how they will accomplish the assignment, what's required and who needs to be part of it
- Meet regularly to ensure everyone is meeting expectations

One last note, bring your entire team together as often as you can. It builds morale, teamwork and leadership. It also gives your team a chance to see the world from other people's perspective.

We've had team sessions where people that had been working at the same company for years but had never taken the time to understand each other's role in the big picture had a chance to talk one-on-one. It's amazing to see them talking and hearing things like "I had no idea you did that".

When your people don't know what is expected of them they will decide for themselves what is acceptable. You may assume they know, but until you're sure they know it's a recipe for anger, frustration and resentment.

It's easier to take the time up front to set clear expectations than to clean up the mess later.

As always if you need help with any of these steps we are just a phone call or email away. We look forward to talking with you.

23
HOW TO GET THE BEST SURVEY RESULTS FROM YOUR EMPLOYEES

We receive a lot of inquiries from business owners on how to best perform Employee Feedback Surveys, or better known as a 360 Degree Surveys. This is a process traditionally wrought with uncertainty and potential dangers. We have seen many employee and management surveys executed over the years. Some have produced promising effects on an organizational culture, and some on the other hand have had devastating results.

Before you undertake in any such exercise we beg of you to first consider the true desired outcomes and context behind why you want to take this step. Is it to be considered an opportunity to involve your staff in contribution towards a powerful future and improved engagement, or a hidden mandate to perform a ritual manager bashing and condemnation session?

In our experience the best way to solicit honest and direct feedback is to do it live, during business hours with committed teams of people. You outlay openly and honestly your intentions and the owner or executives give the opening message.

Develop a feedback system where people have an opportunity to comment openly and truthfully about what is possible for the company, their department, the management style and what improvements they would want to see. Ask them about the roles they want to play and how they want to be considered in business planning. Do not make this about problem solving or complaining, but instead about reflection and ideas to improve operations, communications and efficiencies. **Set the right stage for this work first**.

We could write pages and pages on this topic, but for sake of time, let us share with you a survey format we have found works best with our clients.

Your Feedback Matters – *Company Name*

Employee Feedback – Building a Stronger Team

Your opinion and feedback to make us a stronger, more competitive team is important.

Please help us improve.

1. How do you feel you are included in decisions made that impact your area of work?
2. How do you feel we could better communicate as a team?
3. What specific requests do you have of your manager or the owners to make your work place more productive?
4. How do you feel your department could operate more efficiently?
5. What role would you want to play in improving operations?
6. What do you like the most about working at *company name*?
7. What specific things are you doing in your department that could be shared with others to improve how we work?
8. What are some work-related challenges that you would like to see addressed in the next few months?
9. Employee comments: (feedback encouraged)

Our advice is to keep this process simple, direct and to the point. Get dialogue going quickly amongst people in the group. Allow everyone the opportunity to write out their responses to each question at the beginning of the meeting. Ensure the responses will remain confidential, although if you follow this questioning model, the tendency to criticize and condemn is minimized. The context is about a real future, not just a reflection of past issues. You will definitely be amazed with how communications and transparency will improve just from this first step.

Some people elect to have the surveys completed on-line. People can go into a web service and complete the feedback at their convenience. If you want to take this route, we recommend keeping the results timely with feedback dialogue happening less than 24-48 hours after the survey. If you have the technology on site, keep the exercise to business hours please.

We suggest this not be left as a yearly exercise but planned out at least quarterly. You see, the best companies we work with recognize people as contributors and involve every employee in the chance to be heard on a constant basis.

Please do not take this process lightly. If you are planning this process for your company and want to run this by us first please drop us a note and we can help you walk through our experience.

24
MOTIVATION? LET'S GET THIS STRAIGHT

It happened again, and we can't figure it out. Neil was having a nice lunch with a client, when a local business owner approached his table. Using photos in our marketing is obviously paying off, as this gentleman recognized him right away.

"Hey you're that coaching guy aren't you." He said.
"Yes I am". Neil replied innocently.
"Well, can you motivate me?" He asked.

By this time, our client sunk slowly under table knowing the verbal reply that was to ensue.

Neil's response came swift and direct. *"Why would you need someone to motivate you?"* he replied. *"Why don't you motivate yourself instead of relying on others to do it for you?"* the visitor stood for moment, almost stunned, while our client made a more formal introduction.

Neil's human relations skills were in need of some polishing, but we wanted to make a point and explain what he really does as a strategic coach.

For a number of years now, we have been studying countless books and training programs on the science and behaviours behind motivation. We think it is time to set the record straight behind this 'motivation thing'. To most people (either writing or reading this endless array of stuff) it is apparent that the thinking norm revolves around 'one person needing to motivate another'. We don't get it. In the past few years, have you noticed the sudden and dramatic extinction of those motivational speaking types? There is an obvious reason for their disappearance. We have seen hundreds of examples where people file off to the 'one day pump-up sessions' (ourselves included) only to get all wired up and driving home ready to take on the world. One problem; the next morning you're all fired up walking into work and you don't know why. Worse yet, the people around you are wondering what is wrong with you.

Even the great grandfather of motivation speakers, Zig Ziglar was quoted saying, *"Motivation does not stick, and neither does a bath. That is why you should motivate yourself."*

There are number of good one day programs out there run by amazing people. What we hear most often by local business owners, is how it rarely transfers back to the organization. The difficulty lies in people wanting to be fixed, influenced or even changed by the seminar. This approach rarely produces any lasting effect. To best utilize these programs have the participant return and teach others what they learned. The key here is what they have learned. Have the entire group make a commitment to the business and each other with accountability. Pick one or two things that stood out from the program and ensure they are used by everyone. Link the learning back to the strategy and goals of the company. Your role as an owner or manager is to ensure this expectation is clear and you have created an environment 'hungry' for the learning.

Confucius said, *"I hear and I forget. I see and I remember. I do and I understand."*

The truly great motivational seminars offer tools and ideas that can be transferred back to the company. They are not quick 'one day' fixes, but part of a larger learning strategy. The facilitator drives commitment and is held accountable for measured results. Motivation rarely is spoken in the same line as learning.

Now let us discuss your role as a leader.

As a leader, manager or business owner, your ONLY role in motivating your team is to create the environment that allows people to motivate themselves. They already came to you motivated. You need to keep them from becoming de-motivated. This is not always easy, but critical if you wish to have your best team members hang around for very long.

Here are four key practices to follow:

☑**Listen more than you speak.** People become motivated when listened to and feel like a contributor.

☑**If people are truly motivated, they will stop at nothing to exceed their goals.** You will see it in their actions and results, not just words.

☑**Put your hose away.** If all you are doing is fire fighting, all you will ever produce is fires. There is no motivation in handling urgent items, only burn-out.

☑**Link all seminars and training back to the company through a culture of 'ongoing learning'.**

How about that business owner at lunch? He later told Neil he appreciated his honest approach and asked to give him a call to work with his full team.

25
CONFIDENCE IS CONTAGIOUS

Confidence is attractive, magnetic and a major key to sales success. Ultimately selling is the transference of confidence. You're transferring your belief and ability in what you can do for someone else.

As buyers we want to work with someone who know their stuff. Who we believe will take care of everything. That we made the right choice.

But we've found that many people who are in a sales role lack confidence.

Why?

We guess the first question is where does confidence come from?

Confidence comes from experience and knowing that you can do something well. It also comes from not being afraid to fail.

When someone is new to sales the thing they need most, but lack the most is confidence. This is also true of sales people who may have experience, but are starting a new position at a new company. We've also found that many entrepreneurs lack confidence primarily because they're great at making things, but the selling scares them.

We can't give you a formula to build confidence, but we can ask some questions to ensure you are on the right path.

1. Do you and your sales people have a plan for success? Are you making sure they're doing the right things to be successful? While we don't believe sales is a "numbers" game, we do believe that you need to be doing the right things on a consistent basis to see success. How do you know they are?

2. Do you have an environment that encourages failure? What we mean is are people afraid to take chances or are they encouraged to innovate and to push?

3. Do you and your people have access to successful role models and mentors? Do they know what success looks like? Do they know where to find success stories?

4. Are you and your team consistently working on your selling skills? Are you getting feedback from prospects and customers? Are you reading, watching or listening to new ideas and concepts to improve?

Two other key ingredients into developing confidence are **Time** and **Action**. You need to be patient and nurturing with new sales people and with yourself. You will make mistakes. You will lose sales, but you will also learn. Are you spending enough time with your people? Are you providing learning opportunities or are you just telling them what to do? Remember we learn the most from our mistakes.

When we're in a funk sometimes the best thing to do is start moving. Action breeds confidence. By taking positive action everyday you will start to feel more in control and less timid. Celebrate your small wins but keep pushing.

26
BUSY IS A DANGEROUS WORD

Busy – the new four-letter word.

How many times have you answered the question "how's business" or "how's it going at work" with "Oh, I'm so busy"?

Stop it. Busy can and will kill your business.

Over the last 10 years almost every business owner, CEO, manager and sales person we've coached has asked for help with his or her time management. But there is no such thing as time management. We all have the same amount of time. The challenge is what you do with it.

Being busy means you are reactive. And being reactive means you let things happen to you. If you let time happen to you, then you will always struggle.

What we've found that works is that you need to prioritize. This way you become proactive and you decide what you will do with your time.

Now we can hear your comments. "Sounds great but what am I supposed to do when a customer calls with an emergency, or my staff needs me or a vendor has an issue. I can't just ignore it".

Well, you're right and wrong.

Being proactive doesn't mean ignoring problems or emergencies, what it means is you have the choice.

Busy is a choice. Being reactive is a choice.

Do you have to be the one to handle the crisis, or can someone on your staff? Will the world end today if you don't take care of that issue this minute? Again, these are all choices.

We all have things come up during our day that were not planned. The challenge becomes do we let these interruptions dictate how we use our time.

Also when we react to situations we tend to make emotional decisions and they're usually not the best decisions.

So with all this said, here are three suggestions.

1. Schedule two times a day to read and respond to email – morning and afternoon.

2. Tell your staff they are only allowed to present you with a problem when they have come up with at least three solutions to solve it, two of which include them. (Be prepared to see your staff less).

3. Shut your door for at least one hour a day. It's ok. You need time to think and being distracted doesn't let you think. Schedule this time, and do one thing... think about your business.

27
HEY KIDS, ITS STORY TIME

As human beings we will almost always take the path of least resistance. What ever is the easiest is what we shoot for.

Does this mean we're lazy? Does this mean we don't care?

Well in a nutshell, sort of.

How many times have you asked someone why he or she didn't do what they said they would, only to hear...

"I wanted to work out, but..."

"I tried to get the report done, but..."

"I called the prospect, but..."

Hey everyone gather round, it's story time! Tell me another one please. Excuses – the great killer of action and the killer of ideas and progress.

We're all guilty of this. As a matter of fact it's rampant across many companies. We have good intentions, and then we don't live the commitments we made.

Why?

One of the toughest things to do is to hold yourself accountable. It's way too hard. We are really good at coming up with excuses and because we came up with them, we believe them, act on them and then justify them.

So what can you do?

Here's an idea: **Accountability Partners**

As we said holding yourself accountable is next to impossible. An accountability partners job is to hold you accountable to meet your commitments. They don't do the work for you or help you do the work. They hold the mirror up to you and ask "Did you do what you said you would do." If you did, great what's next? If you didn't they ask you a one word question – why?

At the same time you're helping your partner to live their commitments.

No more excuses. Keep your word. And take "but" out of your vocabulary.

28
THERE IS NO SUCH THING AS TIME MANAGEMENT

In our role as business consultants we hear many, many excuses. My favorite is "I didn't have time".

That one is great because you're not only lying to us, you're lying to yourself.

24 hours. We all have the exact same amount of time every day. It's what we do with that time that makes the difference.

Stop trying to manage time. You can't. It keeps moving with or without you. You can never run out of it. Never accept "I didn't have time" from your staff or yourself again.

Instead of time management work on 'priority management'. When you set priorities you do two things:

- Make your life less complicated
- Make your life less reactionary

When we're constantly in a reactionary mode, we feel busy, productive and important, but in reality we're just spinning in circles. Yes sometimes emergencies happen that demand our attention, but not everyday. By setting priorities we can build our businesses the way we want to vs. with excuses.

Here are some questions to help you determine your priorities.

- Will this make us money?
- Do I have the capability to do this (you or your staff) or do I need help?
- Will this benefit my customers?
- What will the impact be on my business?
- Can this wait?

Another great thing about focusing on priorities is that the little things that eat up a lot of our time as business owners and managers go away because they really weren't that important to begin with.

29
HONEY...ARE YOU READY FOR YOUR PERFORMANCE APPRAISAL?

A number of years back we made a declaration to abolish yearly performance appraisals with our clients. Since then, we have punched our way out of Human Resource offices all over Ontario. This concept, even today, seems so radical and insane that it now requires even further due diligence.

In short, we are not against performance dialogue, but something more powerful instead of the traditional, old-fashioned flogging and brow beating that can only be compared to the Spanish Inquisition. In EVERY company we have ever worked with, the viewpoints people share regarding a so-called manager judging performance is about as enjoyable as a 3 day tax seminar. What's even funnier is most managers just hate doing them and being forced to comply with company policies from the 1990's.

You see no one has ever given you the right to judge another human being...NO ONE! Have you ever noticed the resentment and apathy you feel after having to perform one of these rituals? Pssst, it may have everything to do with you. You see, people will thrive in an environment where they can judge themselves, their performance and contribution to the organization. They own their work, not you. (For more on this topic please see our section 'The Paper Lion'.)

For this chapter, we would like to offer a new context point of view.

Imagine if you might how a typical performance appraisal conversation might happen at home

Honey, can you join me in the living room please. We have been married now for just over a year and I would like to take this opportunity to provide you some constructive feedback and criticism about how you have been doing. It is now a good time to go through your performance appraisal.

You have done some good things this year BUT I would like to give you some feedback about some things I have observed. You may remember back in the summer, you slept in and once you even forget to get the yard work done. You tried to tell me what happened but I need to show you some of your faults. Please do not take this the wrong way, but I am trying to give you ways to be a better spouse.

I know you can be better so lets agree on some ways in which you can improve…OK, here is my ranking system, let's go through it together shall we…

Does this sound extreme? If you have been in as many appraisals as we have, you may start to agree with us. Let us share with you, that if we tried this with our amazing spouses, or partners we would definitely find ourselves renting space in a basement.

For the past 10 years our colleagues and we have been working on better ways to engage people in the performance and learning process. We have developed tools and resources that will help you. There is a better way. Let's talk.

SECTION THREE: **BUSINESS DEVELOPMENT**

Over the past decade we suspect nothing has changed faster in your organization than business development. Gone are the days of trial closes, cold calls and talking about your client's golf pictures to build rapport.

The sales landscape has changed and unless you're prepared you will be doomed to compete solely on price, because in the absence of value price becomes the decider.

Professional sales teams now utilize the web, blogs, social media, and technology. Although these new tools are important, we still recommend and advise traditional methodologies such as advertising, print and networking groups. Having a balanced and strategic approach is the key.

Today, our clients, associates and colleagues all agree that their number one business objective is growing sales. The problem is their customers have more options and it is so much easier to access to information than ever before. Your customers are savvy and are (or feel they are) as educated as you about your products and service.

Your reputation and references are found at a glance and key stroke. So what are people saying about you and your company? How are you standing out in the crowded market? How do you handle praise or complaints? You are expected to be available and accessible 24/7. There is no way around it.

This means you have to do more than just sell products and services.

In the following chapter we will lay out some hard hitting realities for you to consider. We will also provide ideas and actions steps to ensure you are taking advantage of opportunities for growth. There are concepts to capture low hanging fruit and strategies to lead your market place.

30
THE INVENTION OF YOUR SALES EDGE

We're against most theoretical models of selling. So are most salespeople we meet. Traditional models are good points to start from...period. There are plenty of sales models, theories, and advice out there; and just as many 'sales experts' pontificating the value of these models.

Anything we have ever done in the past rarely works with the same success today.

Learning the fundamentals of selling is important. The key lies in moving from theory alone to unique application.

Why follow what everyone else is doing? What makes you unique and different to your customers? Really! **It's you, not a model!!** Rarely do we see salespeople building themselves to be truly different in a marketplace full of clones.

How about asking a prospect what business issues they are facing in today's global economy? What keeps them awake at night? Where is the money hidden within their organization? There are tons more. The key here is how important it is for **sales people to become business people** who think about profits and markets instead of product peddling.

Here is a test. How do you show up on stage in front of your customers? How do you know? What is your competition saying about you? What really makes you different? And what is your plan to be different tomorrow?

The business of selling is changing quicker than ever imagined. Just try to get someone on the phone to start with. Once on the phone you have less than 5 seconds to get their attention....actually most people will make up their mind about you in less than 3 seconds.

So what happened to that traditional 60 second 'elevator speech' allowing you to explain your product?

It is time for action, not theory. It's time to build **YOUR** Sales Edge. You do need to know that you can't do this on your own. Work with someone who will truly bring out **YOUR** strengths and expertise, not give you theirs. Become known as: "You really need to talk to this person; they are really different and are a sustaining resource to my company. Here is his/her number...and here is the phone."

Let's talk about this....

31
GROWING YOUR SALES

There are four primary ways to grow sales:
1. Add more customers
2. Sell at a higher price
3. Encourage customers to buy more often
4. Encourage customers to buy more items/services each time they purchase

So what this means is there are two ways to grow:
1. Find new customers
2. Grow existing customers

If we look at the four points above, three of them are focused on growing existing customers, while only one is about finding new customers. But many, many small business owners spend most of their marketing dollars and energy on finding new customers. If you've been in business for at least a year, you're sitting on a great asset; your customer database.

Don't have a database?

Get started today, you'll need it.

Believe it or not, good customers, you know the ones that you actually make a profit from, don't mind providing you with information, providing you respect it.

Not only are we all business owners and managers, but we're also customers. We buy stuff everyday. We know that when we find a business that we like, and that fulfills our needs we don't mind giving them some information. In fact, we expect it.

The better they know us, the better they'll service us and the happier we'll be. And your good customers are the same.

You need to learn about how they buy, why they buy, how often they buy and how much they spend. Learn about their lifestyle and get ideas about what else you can sell them. How many times have you heard a customer say "I didn't know you sell that... too bad I just bought one last week, if I'd only known."

Now this is probably sounding like a lot of work. We know you have a ton on your plate already. Think of it this way. The only reason your business exists is to find and keep profitable customers. If you're doing something else, then it's not a business it's a hobby.

Collecting and storing a customer database is work, but it's one of the most profitable things you can do for your business. You need to start talking to, listening to and understanding your customers now, or you'll lose them to someone who will.

You can keep focused on finding those new customers; hopefully you'll never run out. But you'll spend more and more money with fewer and fewer positive results. Look at it this way; you've already spent a lot of money finding new customers, isn't it worthwhile to try and keep them?

32
TRUST: THE LOST ART

Over the last 10 years the Internet and social networks have completely changed the way people buy. They can get as much information as they want about any product or service in the comfort of their own home, on their terms and without speaking to a single person.

Sales people existed because they were the primary way consumers could get all of the information they needed. This is no longer the case.

We work with dozens and dozens of sales teams every year. The reason they call us is because they are not reaching their goals like they used to. We have identified three reasons why:

1.   Prospects are harder to reach

2.   There is more noise in the marketplace than ever before

3.   The individuals on the sales team don't bring additional value to the table

The last point is the hardest for them to grasp and the most important.

You see sales people like to pride themselves on product knowledge. While product knowledge is still important, it is the easiest for prospects to get themselves, but it's also the easiest thing for sales people to learn and focus on.

So what are your potential customers really looking for?

Someone they can trust. Yes, trust. It's the number one thing your prospects are looking for.

Chances are someone can buy what you sell from multiple sources, either online or through bricks and mortar. There are just too many choices today and you can no longer simply click on your open sign and wait for your register to ring.

I don't know if people are smarter today, but they sure have access to more information. The problem is they don't know what information to trust. The opportunity for today's sales people is to become a trusted resource that prospects can count on.

It starts with having a give first attitude. What separates great sales people from average is that they help and give away their knowledge and expertise even if they can't directly benefit from it.

We've heard from numerous sales people about how they need to make sales now and can't wait for relationships to foster. First of all if you're focused on is sales and not creating life long customers you will be in trouble sooner than you think. Second, it's not just about relationships, it's about positioning yourself as a trusted resource. It's about building credibility in your market and becoming known for something.

It doesn't matter what type of sales you're in from retail to services, from manufacturing to tourism you can position yourself to your target market. The main thing to keep in mind is that this isn't a strategy or a tactic; it's a sales philosophy that must become part of everything you do.

Here are five things you can do to get started:

1.   Decide what you want to be known for. When you look at successful people they are known for something; they stand for something. What do you stand for? What do you want people to think of when they think of you?

2.   Understand what's really important to the people you want to help. What are the top questions you get asked or that cause the most anxiety for your market?

3.   Create content to share your knowledge, expertise and experience without expectation of return.

4.   Keep your word.

5.   Work at this everyday. There are no short cuts.

You have the opportunity to use technology to your advantage by using it to give trusted advice and extra value to the people you want to serve. Your competitors are most likely not doing this, so the opportunity is even greater.

So don't wait for the perfect time of year to start this because that will never come, just get started today and soon you will see results you haven't realized before.

If you need help with this for yourself or your sales team don't hesitate to call us.

33
WHY SHOULD SOMEONE BUY FROM YOU VS. YOUR COMPETITOR?

This is a very difficult question to answer.

There are so many choices available today and when everything starts to seem the same, price becomes the deciding factor.

In the absence of value, price is the decider. We have used this term often in our writing for a specific reason......it's important. Get it?

Are you giving your customers a better reason to buy from you than your competitors are?

Let's start with your competitive advantage. From the list below which one of the following do you feel is your competitive advantage?

1. Quality
2. Service
3. Knowledgeable staff
4. Selection
5. Location/Hours
6. Reputation
1. Innovation
2. Trust

How many of your competitors are saying the same thing?

Believing that one of the above is a real competitive advantage is a lie many business owners tell themselves. Admitting you don't know your company's true competitive advantage is a big step. But the biggest step is investing the time to figure it out.

To determine your competitive advantage, answer this question:
What can you deliver better than your competitors on a consistent basis that matters to your customers?

So how do you avoid the competing on price trap?

Answer these questions:
- Why should someone buy from you over your competitor?
- What does someone get from you that they don't get from your competitor?
- What can you deliver better than your competitor?
- How important are these differences to your customers?
- Why should your customer care?

Tough questions, but necessary.

Now we're sorry to tell you this but your business is not unique? We know you think it is, but it's not.

You see, almost every business thinks it's unique, but it's not.

Why?

Have you heard of a USP – Unique Selling Proposition? This is where you find something about your business that is unique to your business versus your competitors and you focus your selling and marketing message around this perceived advantage? It must be a benefit to your customers and not easily copied.

That's no easy feat.

It's very rare that we've seen this accomplished. Oprah did it, and then came Dr. Phil, Ellen etc. FedEx did it and then came UPS. McDonalds did it then came Wendy's, Burger King etc.

You see many companies found something unique about them, but in the end they were all copied. So their USP was not so unique.

What you need to focus on is your SSP; Sustainable Selling Proposition. This is where you identify what is most important to your customers when they buy what you sell. Then you build a customer experience that delivers around those reasons.

Study your customers. Study your competitors. Study your suppliers. Learn what your customers perceive as value and what they could care less about. Build a complete experience that makes the customer feel that you know them and understand them.

If you can do this, you have created your SSP, and customers will reward you with repeat purchases, referrals and profits.

34
YOUR SOCIAL JUDGE AND JURY

"You are ALWAYS on stage...people are staring at you and making judgments...so how are you showing up?"

For over a decade we have been asking clients to become aware of how they are showing up on stage in front of others? This is perhaps one of the most difficult questions to answer as only a rare few really understand how they appear to others, judges and critics.

With the advent and exponential growth of social media this question is more important than ever.

Every day you are being stared at by your **family**.
Every day you are being stared at by your **colleagues and peers**.
Every day you are being stared at by your **existing customers**.
Every day you are being stared at by your **potential customers**.
Every day you are being stared at by your **competitors**.
Every day you are being stared at by **the public**.

You are being judged by what others see of you every day. This is a fact.

Some people out there will call it branding; we tend to call it intention.

In business this means you need to make a conscious decision to take control of how others will see you. Social media has made that task very easy....and inexpensive. So what are you posting and contributing to your community that matches how you want to be seen? This is a valid question.

Are you seen as a product peddler, spammer, self centered or a value provider, thought leader, or innovator?

And for those of you out there still not involved in social media and business leadership, there are still judgments being made about you.

There was an old Rush lyric that said, 'If you choose not to decide, you still have made a choice." The same is true for your on-line reputation. Whether you choose to lead or not, there are still judgments being made. Are you willing to take control of your social reputation before the jury returns on you?

35
ABC IS NOW ABQ

We were at a clients' today to meet one of their new sales people. During the conversation the topic of "closing" came up, specifically how closing has become harder and harder in today's environment. It reminded us of an old saying in sales "A-B-C, **A**lways **B**e **C**losing". This archaic thinking is not only out of date; it's probably costing you sales.

Closing is a 1982 sales technique. We guarantee you that the people you're selling to are very aware when you attempt your "trial close" and it pisses them off.

Closing happens when you have presented a value based offering to a problem/opportunity your prospect is prepared to take action on.

Instead of ABC, we believe in ABQ "**Always Be Qualifying**".

What is qualifying?

- Understanding your prospect's needs – can you actually meet them?
- Understanding your prospect's sense of urgency – do they need it now or can it wait?
- Understanding your prospects level of commitment – if you do something are they willing to do something?

- Understanding the hierarchy of the business – who needs to be involved in the decision?
- Understanding how your prospect determines value – do you understand their expectations?
- To be successful in sales you need to spend time with people that want, need and are willing to pay for what you are selling.
- Many of us spend too much time with individuals that are not ready to buy, don't have the authority or don't value our offering.

Sales cycles are longer, there is more competition and your prospects have more demands on their time than ever before. So your job is to qualify them and determine how much time you're willing to commit to each prospect.

As sales people we want to hold on to any glimmer of hope that a prospect will turn into a sale. We want to believe that if we just stay with it, it will turn into a sale. Now we're huge believers in persistence. In fact we've pursued a prospect for up to a year before winning the first sale. But we made sure that we had qualified them and then spent the appropriate amount of time and energy to move the sale along. It's ok if the prospect says no. No is not forever.

Focus on building your funnel or pipeline or list (what ever you want to call it), but be sure to keep qualifying your prospects each time you make contact. Remember their priorities can change in a minute and that hot lead can turn ice cold over night, or just the opposite, they could be ready to buy.

So remember 1982 was fun, but it's now 2014 and closing is dead. Focus on giving value, being professional and qualifying your prospects and you will win more business.

38
TOUCHING YOUR TARGET MARKET

If you are like most owners and sales professionals, you are looking for ways to grow your business development, capture new customers and grow market share. It seems people are now coming out of this economic downturn and realizing **new sales is a priority**. You can no longer rely on your existing client base to grow the way you want. (You have probably already developed their relationship to capacity....right?) The pressure is on and you want to stay ahead of your competitors. Ready, set....GO!

Wait a minute, before you head out with your traditional sales tools, we need to caution you that the rules have changed and getting attention is harder than ever before. People are overwhelmed, attention spans are short, we are flooded with marketing images, people are critical of pitches, e-mails are out of hand and the lists of distractions are endless. **So how do get attention today?**

Even if you have a prospect in front of you, you have less than 10 seconds to make an impression, get attention and provide your value proposition. If your message is solely about you and your product, you are shut down immediately. Where is the 'value' to your customer in your value proposition? *(For more resources on value propositions please contact us.)*

In talking with most sales producers, the sales cycle (time required to take a client from introduction to billing) is much longer than ever before. We hear stories of what used to take days now becoming weeks, months and even years. Wow, you had better fill up your pipeline; it is going to be a long, tough and rough ride.

Our research over the past few years has revealed that to get attention today will take a minimum of 12 touches with a prospect.

Here is the kicker; most sales people give up after 3-5 attempts!

So what are touches you say? Touches are the various ways you and your company can stay on your prospect's radar and in their heads. If you consider a touch a brochure solely about you, your products and how good you are you are going to struggle with this and most likely end up in the trash. A touch is something the prospect would consider of value and a resource for what they are trying to accomplish.

Here are 4 examples of touches we have seen used by local leading edge companies.

1. An industry article with useful business tools that **you** have written that your prospects can apply.
2. An invitation to a resourceful seminar, meeting or workshop run by **you** that your prospects want to attend.
3. A whitepaper, written by **you**, on upcoming industry and market changes and ways your prospects can prepare.
4. An invitation to receive valuable tips by signing up to **your** e-zine or blog.

Note: *If you do not have the resources, energy or time to develop your own material, you can use an industry expert's work. Caution: Just be prepared to lose the business to them.*

We have developed a list of 12 ways to touch your prospect customers. If you want a copy of that list, please contact us and we will send it over to you.

To execute your plan properly you will need a 'touch campaign' and a clear structured strategy.

Potential 12 Touches for Today's Market
- Happy Birthday e-mail
- Article from newspaper
- Personal introduction
- Thank You notes
- Industry trade shows and meetings, invite them to meet
- Technical paper or web link of interest and relevant to customer
- New promotion , sales rep personalize, remind
- Personally deliver and order for your customer
- Phone call, How's it going, status of business

- Phone call, discuss recent success, recommendations
- Follow ups to re-enforce previous touches
- Check their website. Awards, news. Send a note of recognition
- Networking, events, workshops, social settings
- Industry expert meeting or introduction. Organized by you.
- Newsletters
- E-Zines
- Introduce your customer to a potential customer for them, that you know, establish a connection
- Client Appreciation Event, open house, BBQ
- Social Media, LinkedIn, Facebook, Twitter

We are sure there are more we could add to this list. If you have any suggestions please let us know.

37
FOCUS ON YOUR CUSTOMERS FOR THE TRUTH

In today's business market, we see many organizations working hard to grow their market share, sales and team. We are sure you will agree that the very strategies that got us to this point may not take us to where we want to go.

For all of us, the way we see ourselves and our business is limiting at best. Most of us do not really know how we are perceived in the market because we have just worked with ourselves too long. Those companies that continue to re-work old strategies and not seek innovative ways to build their image, offering and service are in serious trouble.

Our commitment is to provide you with ideas that will keep you one step ahead of your competitors and allow you to see your business differently than you see it now.

For years in our consulting work, we have seen good organizations deciding to re-connect with their customers for a serious look at the reality of their image and how they can improve. We have been running Client Focus Meetings together.

Here is how a **'Client Focus Meeting'** works.

Step One:
Invite 6-10 of your key customers to join you and your leadership team for an afternoon or evening session off site and away from your office. Provide them with food and refreshments. Invite customers with varied

backgrounds and relationships to you. (big vs. small, new vs. older, existing vs. lost)

Preface the invitation by asking for their help and honest feedback.

Step Two:

Set up a table in the front of the room for your guests and have your team sit across from them in a horseshoe fashion.

ALL your key stakeholders are in the room and smart phones are off.

Your assignment is to do one thing.....LISTEN. When we say listen, we mean listen for what is possible, not probable based on history. Listening from your 'past' in this exercise is useless.

Step Three:

Involve an outside facilitator to engage your customers and direct the meeting. Ask your key relationships to answer each of the following questions:

1. **Why did you originally decide to do business with us? What brought you to our organization?**
2. **Why do you decide to stay with us and keep doing business?**
3. **What are 3 things we can do to improve our service and relationship with you?**

Step Four:

Please 'truly listen' to what is being said to you. Take notes and ensure each team member is engaged in this process.

Immediately after the meeting, you must commit to making changes based on your customer's feedback. Thank your customers for their honest dialogue and communicate to them what changes you are going to make.

You will have in your possession a clear message about how you are viewed and what is next in your strategic development. This is just one step in gaining your competitive edge.

Last year, our team took the opportunity to run a focus meeting with our key client relationships. The feedback we received was pure gold to our organization and what was possible for us. We had to leave our egos and pride at the door, and by doing so, we were open for receiving the truth and reality about how we are really seen in the market. As an organization, we will never look back.

By involving your customers in your strategic planning and business development process, you are gaining an edge and strengthening relationships all for the cost of a lunch or dinner. We would say that is a good investment.

Depending on the size of your company and its players, you may want to adjust the Client Focus Meeting as needed. Please contact us to discuss the format that will work the best for you.

38
EXCUSE ME IM TRYING TO INTERRUPT YOU

A consumer behavior study was completed in 1978 which indicated that the average North American was exposed to about 2,000 selling messages a day. That number seems overwhelming. The same group that completed the 1978 study updated their research in 2008 and found that number had grown to 5,000 selling messages a day!

As business owners/managers our job is to find and keep customers. That's why our companies exist. But you can't get a new customer if they don't know you exist. So you need to let them know about you, and how do you do that? Traditionally you interrupted them. You purchase advertising of some kind or cold called and said "hello, we're (insert company name), we specialize in (insert your specialty) and we can help you. Well guess what, there are 4,999 other companies doing the same thing to your potential customer everyday.

How many of those 5,000 messages do you think your potential customer remembers, or even more important; acts on?

The answer is close to zero. How many billboards do you remember seeing on the way to work today? How many radio commercials?

A person only takes action to change something when what they're currently using no longer works. So before someone will pay attention to you, they first have to be interested. They have to have **pain**.

So this means you can't talk about you. You can't talk about your products or services either. Don't talk about your customer satisfaction awards, your longevity, your market leadership or how much you spend on R&D.

NO ONE CARES!!!

You need to talk about one thing. PAIN. The people in the marketplace that have that pain will pay attention to your message, everyone else will ignore it. As human beings we block out information that is not relevant to our current situation, but we let in what is. Here's a test. Have you purchased a car recently? We bet that before you became interested in buying a new car you didn't really notice anything about that car – from advertising to how many of them are on the road. But once you were interested you started seeing that car everywhere as well as their advertising. Your brain lets in what's relevant and blocks out the rest.

This is the main reason you need to market your company everyday, On any given day only a small percentage of the market will be interested in your message. Not to complicate things, but there are also two other factors at work: Urgency and Risk.

While someone may be interested in your message they will only take action if they have urgency. If they do have urgency, they still need to trust (RISK) that you can deliver.

So here is a simple formula for talking to potential customers:

1. **Talk about their pain** (Interest)

2. **Identify the consequences of what the pain can lead to** (Urgency)

3. **Tell what happens when the pain is removed** (no product pitch – talk results) (Urgency)

4. **Let others tell how great you are** (testimonials) (Risk)

5. Offer a no risk opportunity to learn more (Risk)

One last tip. Less is more. Keep your message simple and to the point.

39
YOUR CUSTOMERS CUSTOMER

For most professionals in sales the emphasis has always been placed on excellent customer service and value. Although this is as true today as ever, even more is expected to compete in today's changing market. More and more 'me too' competitors are in the game, many of which are playing the price game, forcing you to either play by the same rules or become quickly extinct.

There is a new way to compete. It is going to take some hard work and it will require your sales people to think and act more like business people. They will also need to understand the real issues your customers face, not just what they think they need....your same old product offering.

We would like to introduce you to a concept called **'Your Customer's Customer'**. We have been applying this methodology with amazing success. Here is how it works.

As a sales team, please identify the top 3-5 business issues your key customers are facing right now in business. (hint....it usually has nothing to do with your product) It is probably safe to say it is cash flow, increased sales and repeat business, handling workload and balance, or reputation that comes from their customers.

Your goal:

- How can you help your customer achieve their business goals and

success?
- How can you help your customer's customer receive an amazing experience that will benefit both you and your client? (You're making your customer's life easier.)

This can be better explained with examples:

A concrete contractor is sourcing landscape, interior design, energy efficiency and home maintenance ideas for their customer, local builders. What do the builders want? Recognition, awards and excellent reputation.

A restaurant supply company is sourcing the best interview questions for restaurant owners to use when hiring new staff. What do the owners want? They want staff that will give above excellent service to their patrons, along with the amazing food....to come back again.

A cleaning supply company is sourcing ideas for their clients to save money through environmental initiatives while allowing them to be seen as 'green' innovators in their field. The cleaning company is being proactive in sourcing the new technologies while allowing their customers to focus on the business. (Note. They are also blogging the ideas and adding updates to their LinkedIn accounts....you know, that whole social media gig.)

An insurance broker is offering resources and tools to parents who have children learning to be new drivers. The insurance company is taking the initiative to get the information to the public, many of which are not customers....yet.

With these examples in mind, how can you and your sales team strengthen the relationships you have? We are sure you will agree that customer expectations are higher and more demanding than ever before. How can you be more innovative than your customers and beat your customers to the punch?

These are fair questions.

We are here to help if you are ready.

40
WHATEVER YOU DO, DON'T DO THIS

When the economy slows and consumers start to hold on to their cash a little tighter, many small businesses make a big mistake. When a sales person, either in retail or direct sales, is faced with sales resistance, many of them have an initial response to ask "would you buy if the price was lower?"

This is a big mistake, and one you may never recover from.

Price-cutting is a bad idea. Many industries have created a very difficult situation for themselves by always having sales and price-cutting. Most of the people that don't buy because they say your price is too high, are really not buying because you haven't sufficiently demonstrated value.

Cutting price almost never leads to new sales. Unless someone was already planning on buying in the first place, price-cutting doesn't work. Not only doesn't it work, it's also very destructive to your profits.

Example
Product is priced at $100. Your cost is $70 (this is a 30% margin). Because sales are slow you put the product on sale for 20% off so you now sell the product for $80. Your profit is now $10. So a 20% price reduction = a 66% cut in profits.

Now that's bad enough, but here's the really bad part, once you lower the price, you'll find that you need to keep it priced lower to maintain future sales. So your $100 sale is now $80. Cut the price again for the next sale and guess what, your profit is zero.

Believe it or not it gets worse.

The next step is that your competitors now decide to lower their prices. Can you survive a price war? Unless you are the lowest price in a price war, you're helping your competitor sell more.

So here is the scenario you're facing:

3. The economy slows, so customers become more price sensitive and are slower to make buying decisions
4. As you start to feel the sales crunch you decide to offer a price discount
5. Customers that were already going to buy take advantage of the price discount
6. Your profit margins begin to sink, and now you have less money to invest in marketing or in training your people or in improving your products and your overall business
7. Your competitors also lower their price and you have to continue cutting your price until your profits are at zero
8. Unless you are the lowest price you're actually helping your competitor sell more

Not the greatest situation is it?

Price cutting has always been seen as the lazy way out. Management Guru Michael Porter says "cutting prices is usually insane if the competition can go as low as you can."

So what do you do?

Here are three suggestions:

1. Better explain the value of your offering – find out exactly what your customers want and then work to deliver on that.
2. Bundle or package products and services to maintain higher prices
3. Do something special – go to your best customers and create an added value offering to solidify their loyalty

The bottom line is if your business exists strictly as a me-too, you have no choice but to compete on price. Price is only an issue in the absence of value. If you haven't taken the time to truly understand the wants and needs of your customers and to properly demonstrate that you can deliver, then price cutting may be your only option.

It's a lot of work to compete on value, but especially in times of economic uncertainty, it's more important than ever. Remember it's not the product or service and the associated features people are buying; it is the solution to their problem or the satisfaction of a need or want. Focus on that before cutting your price.

41
FEAR

Don't let fear stop you. Fear can be a good thing.

Up until recently I wasn't a fan of cold calling. Not because I didn't think it would work, rather because I had a fear of doing it. I'm not sure why I was afraid, but I was.

I had built it up in my mind that it would be hard to do, I wouldn't be successful and that I would meet great resistance.

The funny thing is I do seminars all the time for various sized groups from 10 to 100, but the thought of calling one person stopped me in my tracks.

My partner Neil Thornton is a master at cold calling. I would listen to the ease of his language and how easily he built rapport on the phone. I have to admit, I found it intimidating, and because of that, I continued to put it off. But what I realized is that I was putting up artificial barriers. I was thinking and believing that I had to emulate my friend and deliver the same style of cold call. The truth is that I needed to create my own style.

So don't let fear stop you, let it motivate you. Trying something new can be exhilarating.

While I'm still not cold calling's #1 fan, I truly believe it is a great sales tool for my business. I work hard to make cold calls on a weekly basis and as a result I have success booking appointments.

The key to a good cold call is the same as the key to a good ad...be relevant. Keep the focus on the person on the other end of the phone and tell them what's in it for them.

SECTION FOUR: **MARKETING**

One of the hardest areas of business to understand and achieve success is the area of marketing. It is a moving target that every business owner wants to grasp.

Every one of your customers is exposed to over 5000 promotional messages a day, including yours. The problem is 99.9% of them are ignored. So how do you stand out from the rest?

"Either become distinct, or become extinct. The choice is yours." Tom Peters

This quote hits home for us. How about you? Like you, we have spent over 20 years developing our brand and influence in the business community and on line. One truth remains. Just when you think you have the game figured out, someone changes the rules. That someone is typically….well always, your customers and competitors.

Over the years we have worked with numerous businesses in the area of marketing and we wanted to share with you what we've learned along the way.

Some trends we have seen include too many small and mid-sized companies wasting thousands of dollars on out dated and tired marketing when there is a better way.

We have seen numerous companies avoiding new marketing media simply because they are satisfied with historical results (which are no longer producing the same results as before) or resist change. Typically a combination of both. They believe that old methodologies will produce improved results. Is this not the definition of insanity?

We have seen companies resting on previous successes, only to be punched in the face by quick and flexible upstarts. A small office with a handful of energetic and flexible entrepreneurs can shake the foundations of behemoth size and history in a blink of the eye.

You do not have to be part of the crowd of companies still dragging around history and ego. This next chapter will challenge your thinking. We do not intend to throw out the baby with the bathwater on your marketing. We believe in a balanced approach of traditional and new media options; yet one thing is certain. You will need to change the way you see yourself and your marketing for your company.

None of us know enough to be a skeptic. If you're open for some new perspectives, then read on. If you think you have the game figured out, get your resume ready for print; you're going to need it.

42
FIVE KEYS TO GREAT MARKETING

A great friend of ours taught us years ago that when you're faced with a challenge, you should put your thoughts into groups of five. It makes it easier to remember complex ideas and it forces us to think it through until we fully understand the issue.

We were thinking about marketing the other day (like we do most days... we're such geeks) and it dawned upon us that most of the small business owners we talk with don't really understand what marketing is. So we thought about it and realized we didn't have a specific definition of our own.

So we put our thinking caps on and came up with this; Marketing is: "how you connect with your market".

Wow nice and simple, not really complicated, but a little vague as well. So again because we like fives so much, we decided to come up with the five keys to great marketing:

1. **Relevant**
a. Is it of interest to your customer?
b. Does it affect their life?
c. Is there a need for this?

2. **Consistent**
a. Can someone recognize your business?
b. Are you there when your customers are ready to buy?

c. Are you presenting the image you want?

d. Can you repeat your successes?

3. **Clear**

a. Is your message simple and easy to understand?

b. Is it easy to buy from you?

4. **Honest**

a. Keep your word

b. Deliver on your promise

c. Listen, learn and act

5. **Actionable**

a. Do you give your customers a reason to act?

b. Have you created urgency?

c. Can you deliver on what you've promised?

No matter what strategy, tactic or idea you're trying to implement, you need to make sure these five elements have been thoroughly thought through and that you understand how they will help you connect with your customers. Great marketing is a combination of common sense, creativity and the ability to listen. Practice these everyday and your customers will reward you.

43
IT'S TIME TO LOOK IN THE MIRROR

No matter what size your company is – one person or 10,000 – you have a brand. And that brand is developed and cultivated over time. It's a combination of your products and services, facilities, staff, online presence and every other little thing in your company that touches your customer in some way.

When you started your company you had a vision or an idea of what your business would be, what it would look like and what it would stand for.

If you've been in business for any period of time, you need to ask yourself: does what I'm known for, match what I want to be known for?

The mirror effect

Your brand is a mirror. It reflects you and what you are and it allows your customers to see something of themselves in it.

People don't like to be sold, they like to buy from people they trust and like. In other words people interact with others that share some of the values and beliefs they have. When a potential customer comes in contact with your brand do they see something of themselves?

Let's look at two giant brands: Coke and Pepsi. Each brand is very distinct from each other, yet they sell similar products. What separates them is how their customers connect and relate to each brand.

Pepsi has an urban and youth appeal while Coke has a traditional and family appeal. Both are fine brand positions, but not many individuals can relate to both. Yes taste has something to do with what people will choose, but they are initially attracted to the brand that most reflects and connects with them as a person.

We know that these are giant brands and they have unlimited funds to establish their position, but you need to understand that how your brand connects with your audience determines how much of an impact price will be in the conversation.

The reason this happens is that most small and mid-sized companies are so identical that their customers can't tell them apart. Because of this their customers believe that each of them basically offer the same thing, so the only differentiator is price.

When your brand is unique and not just different for the sake of being different (our logo is blue, theirs is red), we mean really distinct in specific ways that your customers really care about, you gain a tremendous advantage.

There is some great news. It has never been easier to stand out than it is today. Because you compete in a market of boring me-too companies, you can become the standout. By taking the time to better understand your customers and what's really important to them, you can create a unique offering that will resonate with your customers.

So where do you start?

- Start with understanding where you are today. Have your business mystery shopped as well as your competitors and get a 3rd party unbiased opinion of your offering as it compares to your competitors.
- Have frank conversations with customers you feel will give you honest feedback. Ask them four questions:
1. Why did you decide to do business with us?

2. Why do you continue to?
3. When you purchase what we sell, what is most important?
4. What are three things we could do to make your experience better?

- Ask your staff and suppliers what they hear from customers. Ask them what they think you could do to stand out.

- Once you've identified what's really important to your customers, determine what you want to be known for. But be 100% sure you can deliver on it.

- Have courage. It takes chutzpa to stick your neck out and to be different. You need to give your brand time to build and to let your customers get to know it. Consistency will be your biggest challenge and not going back to the way things used to be.

When you deliver an experience that no one else is, you customers will notice. And if you deliver it exceptionally and consistently they will tell others.

44
THE FASTEST WAY TO LOSE A CUSTOMER

We get asked a lot about price-cutting. This topic comes up even more when the economy is slow.

Let's look at one facet of price-cutting called 'LTV'.

LTV = Life Time Value. This means that a customer is worth more than the value of a single transaction, they are worth a lifetime of transactions.

If a customer typically spends $25 each time they visit your business, and they tend to visit once a month that customer spends $300 a year with you. If you can keep that customer for 5 years, that customer is worth $1,500.

Now let's look at price-cutting. First it typically does not attract new customers. If someone wasn't already looking for what you sell, chances are they're not going to buy. So price-cutting actually cuts the price for someone who was already going to buy. Second, now that this person has received a discount, they will come to expect it, and will be willing to wait until it goes on sale again (see clothing, furniture, cars etc.).

This price cutting strategy has now changed the LTV of that customer. First, their average purchase will now be lower, and the number of times they shop with you per year will be lower as well, as they wait for it to be on sale. Also, the chances of keeping this customer for the 5 years is even more difficult because you've conditioned them to look for the lowest price, which might not always be you.

If you don't want to get caught in the price war focus on these three things:

1. Create a customer experience measurably better than any of your competitors. Look at all of the touch points of your business and determine how you can make the customers experience memorable. Your goal is to get customers talking about you.
2. Provide extra value and don't touch your price. By giving your customers more, even if it's just perceived to be more, will make them feel like they're getting a better deal
3. Thank them. On a regular basis go out of your way to meet your customers and to thank them. We guarantee you no one else is doing this. You will stand out.

45
TO BRAND OR NOT TO BRAND

What is branding?

We get asked this a lot. Some think it means a shiny new logo. Some think it means a new advertising campaign, and some don't have a clue.

Our definition of branding is this:

"The sum of all experiences a customer has with a business that helps him/her form their perception of the company".

So branding is everything. Every interaction a customer has with your business is influencing their perception of your business in their mind.

And when we say everything, we mean everything from your signage, store front, invoices, advertising and social media to how you answer the phone. Every "touch- point" you have with your customers.

So here's the rub. You can brand your company to be what you want it to be, or you can leave it up to chance and let others (customers, competitors and staff) decide what your brand will be.

Think about that for a minute.

You worked incredibly hard to start this business of yours, the long hours, the sweat, the worry and then you let other people decide what you will be known for and how your customers will think about you.

Are you kidding us?

When you started your business you had a vision of what it would be like when it grew up. Are you on your way? Are you sure?

All of us get caught up in the running of our businesses, putting out fires and solving problems. This can cause us to get complacent, lazy and unfocused. The little things can slip by and before you know it you're losing customers and sales are slow or declining.

Branding is a 24 hour a day job. With so many competitors and exceptionally knowledgeable customers you need to stay sharp and on top of "the little things".

So when you look at your business are you sure it's growing up to be what you want it to be or are you just hoping?

Here is a simple 6-step branding recovery plan:

1. Look at your business as a customer would and identify every touch point.
2. For each touch point, determine if you are delivering the value you need to?
3. Make the necessary changes.
4. Make sure all of your people are on board.
5. Get continuous customer feedback.
6. Review this every month.

This will take some time and effort to do, but it is probably the most important thing you could do for your business. Just like with anything else in your business if you need help to get this done, find it, but don't wait another day.

46
WHERE ARE YOU IN THE MIND?

What is your business known for? Is it what you want it to be known for? The bigger question is, are you sure that's what you're known for? You see what a customer perceives is, to them, a reality.

If you believe you are the highest quality producer, but your customers think of you as medium quality but a low price, that's what you are.

What the customer thinks, or believes is real, is what matters.

Let's take a test. Get a piece of paper and write down your answers to these questions:

1. The safest car made?
2. The ultimate driving machine?
3. Toughest truck?

Now because this is in writing you may have cheated and looked at the answers below, but each of these companies have developed a marketing strategy to become known as the statements above. They didn't leave it up to chance.

If you don't have a clear and distinct difference, your customers will do one of two things:

A. Assign you a label based on their experience with your company – could be good/could be bad

B. Ignore you because you are a "me-too" company and therefore irrelevant Look at GM and Chrysler. They're both in trouble and their brands don't mean as much anymore. What is a Pontiac?

The sad thing is that most small businesses are me-too companies and are doomed to a life of struggling for sales, competing almost exclusively on price and diminishing margins.

Companies that take the time to develop a truly distinct marketing strategy have the ability to "own" that space in the customer's mind. When someone wants the safest car made, they automatically think of Volvo. So how do you develop this distinct marketing strategy? Start by answering these questions:

1. What are the most important criteria for your customers when they buy what you sell?

2. Of those what do your competitors already own?

3. Of those that are left what can you deliver on better than your competitors?

4. Create a company wide strategy to deliver on that singular strategy

Remember its all about what is in the mind of the customer. You must first truly understand what is important to your customers and then determine what you can own.

A key to owning a particular position is ability to deliver. Make sure you have the ability and credentials to own that position. The next step is to clearly and consistently communicate it to your customers and prospects. Don't get sucked into trying to be all things to all people, there is no such thing and all you will do is lose.

Answers to the above:
1. Volvo
2. BMW
3. Ford

47
WHAT TO DO WHEN THE ECOMONY SLOWS

The news media are working overtime to scare the hell out of us.

Everyday, all day we hear about a prolonged recession, increased prices and all around fear.

Unfortunately, we can't control what the media says, but we can control our own businesses.

When the economy slows the first thing most small businesses do is cut their marketing and advertising spending.

This is probably the worst and stupidest thing you could possibly do.

Here's why.

1. Your customers will still need goods and services. Maybe they won't buy as often or as much, but they still need things, so if you stop telling them why they should buy from you, they'll find someone who will.

2. If your competitors are like most small business owners they'll cut their marketing and ad spending. This is a great opportunity for you to grab up more business. When the economy slows great businesses grow because

they don't panic, they communicate with the market and provide good value.

3. Cutting your advertising during a market slowdown makes it much harder to recover.

At the same time don't get caught up in heavy discounts and lowering your prices. Reliance on price incentives as a marketing tool is dangerous — it devalues your brand, and it's hard to wean consumers off it.
Here are some things you should do:

• Focus on advertising with clear and proven return on investment, such as internet and promotional advertising.

• Be prepared to cut budget bloaters like trade shows, which have a harder time proving ROI.

• Focus on your brand's core base, instead of going after more expensive new customers.

Note of Interest: In a study of U.S. recessions, McGraw-Hill Research analyzed 600 companies from 1980-1985. The results showed that business-to-business firms that maintained or increased their advertising expenditures during the 1981-1982 recession averaged significantly higher sales growth, both during the recession and for the following three years, than those that eliminated or decreased advertising. By 1985, sales of companies that were aggressive recession advertisers had risen 256% over those that didn't keep up their advertising.

In addition, a series of six studies conducted by the research firm of Meldrum & Fewsmith showed conclusively that advertising aggressively during recessions not only increases sales but increases profits. This fact has held true for all post-World War II recessions studied by The American Business Press starting in 1949.

48
I DIDN'T KNOW YOU DID THAT

You're on the phone with one of your better customers and he's telling you about a problem he recently had and you say, "I can help you with that". But then you hear "Really? I didn't know you did that; I just bought it from ABC widgets. I wish I had known, I would have bought it from you."

How many times have you heard that one? Ouch.

We can't take for granted that our customers know everything we do, even if they've been buying from us for years.

Your customers are busy people. When they interact with you, they're focused on their immediate problem/opportunity. But you still have the chance to let them know what else you do.

So how do you know what to tell them about?

Have a conversation. Every time your customer interacts with your business they are re-evaluating your value. By showing them what else you do and proving your expertise, you further engrain yourself with them.

It also allows you to get to know them better. At the end of the day with all things being equal, people like to buy from people they like and people that they feel understand them.

The first step is for you to be clear about what it is that you do. If you have 400 things you offer you'll overwhelm your customers.

Instead focus on the key problems you solve or the opportunities you help your customers realize. People don't buy products and services, they buy the results.

Once you've clearly indentified how you can help, create simple communications to your customers. Don't tell them about everything at once, instead focus on one thing at a time. This does two things:

- Gives you a reason for consistent communications
- Allows you to spoon feed your information so it has time to sink in

So don't wait another day to get started on this or you'll hear about another customer buying something from your competitors.

49
HEY GRANDMA HERE'S MY LATEST MARKETING BLOG

Social media conversations are all about context not content. Your content is driven by your context.

Confused?

What we're saying is that based on the social media tool you're using (Facebook, Twitter, LinkedIn) you have very distinct people you're communicating with, so because of that your conversations need to be different.

Facebook tends to be friends and family. People must know you in some capacity before they can connect with you and you with them. The types of conversations on Facebook tend to be very social in nature. You usually have some type of history with each of your connections so you can make personal comments, share photos, and you know things they like. You can talk business but you don't want to be "that guy". You know the guy that goes to a friend's party and tries to sell everyone at the party. There's a place for business conversations with friends and family, but it needs to be softer and more general.

LinkedIn is a professional networking site. While you don't have to be stiff, most of the relationships you have here are business based. Your profile is an extension of your company and brand. Your conversations should be more carefully chosen and more focused on business. With Linkedin you need to know the person your communicating with either directly or through the shared credibility of a colleague. Trust is a big component in the relationships on Linkedin.

Twitter can combine both worlds. You don't need to know the person you're following, and you can discuss both business and lifestyle. What you need to remember is that Twitter's strength is in its ability to help people with similar interests connect. This allows you to build a worldwide network of people you don't yet know, but that you can learn from and share with. While there may be a potential for thousands of customers, you don't want to talk about your offerings until you've established credibility and trust. The goal is to share insights, ideas and experiences first.

This is why we don't recommend you send the same message to all three audiences. It doesn't work. You speak differently to people you know compared to people you're meeting for the first time. Also the people you're talking with will have vastly different interest levels in you and what you do.

We're not talking about being fake, or changing your personality. We are talking about knowing whom you're talking to and what would interest them.

We are marketing geeks, and we love talking about it, but we're not going on Facebook to talk with family from Saskatchewan or cousins from Kentucky about marketing because they have no interest in it. And we're not going on LinkedIn to discuss someone's birthday party.

While LinkedIn is a professional network, it doesn't mean we only connect with marketing professionals there. Some of our connections have no interest in marketing, so we need to tailor our message to engage them.

With each of these tools we suggest you decide what you want to be known for and what information you want to share? From there you can create a content strategy for each tool.

We are not the be all end all experts of social media. We like to share our observations and experiences. While this is about how to use social media, it's really about how to talk to people. No matter what you're using to communicate, it starts with understanding whom you're talking to, what they're interested in and how you can connect with them.

We tend to overcomplicate things. At the end of the day it's just one person connecting with another.

50
I'M BEGGING YOU, PLEASE STOP BORING ME

We can't take it anymore.

Everywhere we look all we see is horrible marketing.

"Look at me, I won an award", "Look at me, we have a sale", "Look at me, we have nothing to say". "We've been in business for 35 years" or "We're number one in service". Who cares?

When you are trying to attract someone, do you normally try to bore them to tears, or do you try to help them understand what you have to offer and how it will benefit them?

Larry was recently speaking with a small business owner and she was showing him all of the lovely print ads she had recently placed in some local newspapers. In total she had spent about $2,000 over a six week schedule.

He asked her how the campaign did. She said "I didn't get a single call."

We were not at all surprised.

First of all, she's a new business and has little to no credibility in the market yet. Second, the top third of her print ad was her company name and logo, absolutely no benefit to the reader. And third, she had nothing interesting to say.

It's no wonder the ads were a complete flop.

Each of us is a business owner, but we're also consumers and customers. So for a minute put on your customer hat and think about this.

- How busy are you on an average day?
- How many ads, posters, billboards, radio commercials, TV commercials, internet banners etc. do you think you're exposed to in a single day? (I'll answer that in a minute)
- How many can you remember?

Your customers are just like you. Busy, tired, stressed and focused on their own lives. They share the same pain as you do, and they're proving it by ignoring marketing more and more everyday.

The good news is that marketing and advertising still work, and they can work very well if you would just stop boring people.

So to help you out, here are some simple guidelines to follow.

- Your ad should focus on one thing. Don't try to explain everything you do or everything you have to offer in an ad. Focus on one thing.
- Tell the customer something they will find interesting. Here's a hint, it's not about you, or your awards or your longevity in business. They want to know what you can do for them that will make their day or life better.
- Ask them to do something.
- Make it incredibly easy to contact you. Have a phone, email and web site and if you have a physical location put in your address and hours of operation.
- This is the most important. DON'T BE BORING!!!!!

Believe it or not, but it is much more risky to play things safe than to risk offending someone, or being controversial.

You will never in a million years appeal to everyone in your market. Never. So don't be worried about the people who don't get you or won't buy from you. No matter what you do they still won't buy from you.

If people start talking about you, you win. Ideas that get talked about spread and soon you'll find yourself making money.

(By the way, the average consumer is exposed to between 2,000 to 5,000 promotional messages a day. Think about that the next time you create an ad).

51
SO YOU'VE BUILT A WEBSITE...NOW WHAT?

You've built a website. Good for you.

You've spent countless hours and energy getting everything just right. Your company history, about page, products pages and testimonials pages are skillfully written and the site is optimized so Google will love your rich text.

Nice work.

You've added great photos of your people and products and you've made sure that you have social media icons on every page.

Again... great job.

Now what?

The problem is all you've done is create another brochure. Can you hear your prospects snoring, or worse leaving your website and never returning?

Don't feel too bad, you're not alone, most websites aren't very good.

The reason most websites suck is because they're created either by a web programmer or your company's IT person. (If you're either of these we apologize, but seriously step away from the website).

You need to create a website for the visitor. Your site needs to be intuitive. This means you need to understand what your customer goes through when they deal with you. What works and where the problem areas are.

Before you design anything, here are some suggestions to help you get it right the first time.

- Identify who are you talking to? You need to really understand who is coming to your website.
- What information do they need?
- What questions do they need answered?
- A successful sale usually allows the prospect to take one step at a time so that they feel comfortable and build trust in you with each step. What steps do they need to take?
- What would make them want to come back to your site?
- What content would they consume?
- What forms of media do they like best (video, photo, text, audio)
- How frequently do you need to create it?
- Is it easy to find it?
- What do you want them to do?
- Ask them to take action – but make sure you've earned the right to ask. Be sure you lead them through a logical process, but evoke emotion at each stage to engage them and encourage them to take the next step

While social media continues to grow and businesses continue to increase their presence in them, it's still critical to have your own website. The various social media tools have a degree of ownership of what you put on their sites and can without notice remove some or all of it.

Also having your own website allows you to be in complete charge of your message and how it's delivered.

If you're unsure how to answer the questions we've presented here, take some time to watch and talk to your customers. Learn how they interact with your staff and your products and services. Learn the questions they ask most, what they like best about your business and why they continue to buy from you.

When you really understand your customers your website can become an extension of the experience you're delivering and not some disjointed train wreck.

We are here to help you, so please feel free to connect with us if you want to improve your existing site or build a brand new one.

52
PLEASE LIKE ME

We get asked a lot about using Facebook as a marketing tool for business. Now we're the first to tell those who ask that we're not experts, in fact because Facebook is so large and ever changing that we doubt there are any real experts.

But, here is one thing we know doesn't work.

Begging for likes.

We see companies using traditional media to promote their business and at the bottom of the ad it reads "Please like us on Facebook for more valuable deals".

First let's look at why 'likes' are or are not important.

When someone "likes" your business page, they are giving you permission to communicate with them. Please note we did not say "sell" or "market" to them, we said "communicate".

Social media is about connecting with an individual, not mass marketing. So when someone likes you they are open for a conversation. It's your responsibility to be interesting and relevant to that individual.

Likes are earned.

Many business owners we speak with are more concerned with how many people they can get to like them instead of the conversations they have with them. It's not a race. Your goal shouldn't be to get as many likes as you can. Your goal should be to connect with the people that have taken the time to come your page and interact with you.

Learn from them, share ideas with them and gain insight as to why they buy from you and how to improve their experience. If you do a great job at this, they will spread the word about you and that will build your likes.

Social media is a wonderful tool, but too many business owners don't understand or don't believe that traditional mass media tactics and mindsets don't work here.

Share your knowledge. Give away your insight and experience.

People will like that.

53
WHAT IS YOUR SOCIAL VALUE?

"Are you still using social media to try to sell me something I don't want to buy, or are you giving me value and ideas to solve my problems or hit my goals?"

Our group at Trigger Strategies has been writing and speaking about the business application of social media and the impact it can have on your sales development. We have talked about the danger of overlaying traditional advertising into this new global phenomenon, product peddling and bribing us with deals to 'like' or 'follow' you.....at which time you relentlessly keep flogging us with how great your deals and product are.

PLEASE STOP IT. You are pissing people off. Why? Simply, social media is about listening first, building rapport and providing value, then earning the right to talk about product and solutions.....in that order.

When presenting this philosophy to our clients and colleagues, they all agree with the new rules, but many are still confused about where to start in the world of providing value. The intention of this chapter is to give you some starting points and ideas to work from.

In short, you and your company provide solutions based upon the application of your service. When working with our clients we ask them to recognize the top 3-5 issues their existing or potential customers are facing. The message you send them must revolve around one or a number of these issues and how you can solve them.

Conflict arises when you think that your customers need your product, but in fact they are looking for the SOLUTION your product provides. As an example a pool company does not sell spas, they sell stress relief and family enjoyment. People do not buy the spa, they buy the experience.

Here are some 'value' examples we have dealt with over the past few years. You may recognize what you can now send out in your social media campaign.....not your latest deal or sales pitch. (Don't forget, people care about themselves, not you or your product.)

- If you are in the construction business - **please send me ideas to protect my new wood deck or fence.**
- If you are in the real estate business - **please send me ideas to improve the value of my home.**
- If you are in the travel business - **please send me ideas to better plan my next vacation.**
- If you are in the insurance business - **please send me ideas to better protect my security.**
- If you are in the floral business - **please send me ideas to beautify my home.**
- If you are in the home staging business - **please send me ideas to make my neighbours jealous.**
- If you are in the automotive business - **please send me ideas to best detail my car on the weekend.**
- If you are in the winery business - **please send me ideas on the most beautiful wine routes.**
- If you are in the restaurant business - **please send me ideas on new healthy menu options.**
- If you are in the appliance business - **please send me ideas on how to clean my toaster and fridge.**
- If you are in the recycling business - **please send me ideas on the new e-waste regulations.**
- If you are in any business - **please send me ideas that I can apply to my life situation.**

How often should you send these messages out? We suggest at least weekly. Daily can be too much and monthly is too far apart.

One objection we have heard is that you do not have time to develop all these ideas. Our answer is simple.....'No problem, I am sure the ideas will come from a competitor soon enough if not already." Get it? If you don't have time to develop ideas and solutions for your market, please get out of business as quickly as you can.

When you are able to send value out to your market that arouses eager wants and engages people into action, you have it down.......keep going.

54
LOOK AT ME! LOOK AT ME!

Attention small business owners – stop using social media for self-promotion only.

No one cares.

Yes social media can help you build your business, but not by forcing your self serving messages on the world.

Here is a formula for success in social media:

- Identify who you want to communicate with
- Determine what information they find valuable and how they like to be communicated with
- Start to connect with them on the social platforms they use
- Create, find and share content related to the information they're interested in
- Give them proof that you know what you're talking about
- Join their communities and ask them to be part of yours
- Communicate with them regularly and get to know them
- Once you've earned the right – invite them to learn more about what you do

If you do this you will achieve three things:

- Trust
- Reputation
- Opportunity

No one will buy from you until they trust you. Trust is always the first step in any sales relationship – online or offline.

With the Internet your customers have more choice than ever before. They can buy from anyone at anytime. The culmination of your content and the history of you giving it away establishes you as a leader and an expert. If your customer has more choices, why not show them you really know your stuff. In other words why you're the best choice.

Because you have earned trust and have established yourself as an expert, you now have the opportunity to ask for their business. And if you've done a really good job on the first two (trust and reputation), most of the time you won't even have to ask – they will seek you out.

The two things that small business owners are missing the most as it relates to social media are patience and courage.

Because many business owners don't fully understand what social media is and what it's about, they lose patience and want to fall back on what they know – pushing out sales messages. Building good relationships takes time. Both sides need to get to know each other. You need courage to stick with it and give it the time it needs.

The best part is, because you spent the time to establish yourself as an expert and you've taken the time to learn about the customer and build trust, price will be far less important and the opportunity to keep the customer long term is much greater.

Social media isn't the be-all-end-all, but it is becoming a major part of how all businesses will build their customer base and more importantly keep them.

So the answer is yes. You can build your business and make sales via social media, but you won't accomplish that by pushing self-serving only messages at everyone. Follow the steps above and you'll be well on your way.

55
SOCIAL MEDIA GONE WRONG

We like social media. we like Facebook and LinkedIn, very cool tools. But we do have one major problem with how they're used for business.

The majority of what we see is people using new media with old traditional interruption methods. In the previous chapter, we have referenced traditional marketing often. We felt it worthwhile to dig a bit deeper.

Social media is just that, social. We believe that when you use social media, you should have a give first strategy. Create something very interesting that your friends and connections would find valuable. If it's good they'll come back for more. If it's really good, they'll pass it on.

But what seems to be happening is we're taking the old stuff we used to place in newspapers, direct mail and email blasts and put it on FB, LinkedIn etc.

You can put lipstick on a pig, but it's still a pig.

We need to keep the word social in our minds. Social media is the digital version of meeting someone individually. When we use traditional media we're strangers interrupting strangers. If we're lucky 1 or 2% of those strangers will be interested enough to get to know us a little more.

In the social media world, you already know them and they know you, at least to some degree. So why would you try to bore them to death?

In a face-to-face setting you wouldn't walk up to someone you know and say – here is a bunch of stuff all about me. Me me me! No you engage them in conversation, offer some new information that they might find interesting and get them talking.

This is what social media is all about.

We know we all want to take advantage of this "so called" free media (that's a concept for another day) and build our businesses. But it doesn't work that way. We need to earn the right to someone's attention and interest.

It's no longer all about you. Develop a give first philosophy. Focus instead on creating great content. We're not talking volume – that's what you've been doing. We're talking about content that is well thought out and worth spreading.

One of our favorite authors – Scott Stratten says "people spread awesome".

So starting today, change your ways and make something awesome.

56
SOCIAL MEDIA IS ALL ABOUT
GIVE AND TAKE

Almost everyone we know or meet these days is applying some form of social media in their life. Be it Facebook, LinkedIn, Twitter or whatever the newest thing is.

Some do it for purely personal reasons; to connect with old friends, family or long lost loves.

Some do it strictly for business reasons to connect with customers, vendors, colleagues and potential customers.

And some (us included) do it for both.

No matter what your focus is, there are two sides to social media.

- Taking
- Giving

Sounds simple right? In principle it is.

Taking consists of viewing other peoples pages and posts. Consuming media including photos, videos, audio, text and links.

Giving consists of generating information (content) for others to consume, share and comment on.

No matter what your goal is (personal/business/both) you need to be active in both giving and taking.

Social media is a group of tools to help us connect. The rules of communication don't change because we're using a phone or computer.

In the days before technology we used to take time to get to know people, share stories and to show interest in what they were doing. This is what social media is best at – helping us connect, share and learn.

So when you're ready to dive into social media remember that you can't just be a taker and you can't just be a giver. You need to be a person – be yourself and join the conversation.

57
A TWITTER BUSINESS STORY

In our work with clients, we are constantly asked for the business relevance of social media and how it applies to growing sales and the development of new clients. This is a fair question and best answered by articulating how we connected with one of our largest clients at Trigger Strategies.

Neil was watching a regional news channel one morning and the CAO from a leading financial institution was being interviewed about investment options and changing markets. The advice he was sharing was relevant and valuable. At the end of his segment, people were invited to follow his insights on Twitter.

Looking for more, he quickly connected with him and mentioned how much he liked his interview and how he could apply his advice in our business. By the end of that same day, he replied and mentioned he too had been following Neil's work and asked for some help with a social media strategy and an intern placement for this marketing team.

After some dialogue together through LinkedIn (able to view experience, credibility and recommendations) an initial meeting was set up to talk further. That initial Twitter dialogue was the beginning of what has been a long and beneficial relationship.

Looking back on the past year, we can now say that over 80% of our new business development now stems from social media dialogue and shared interactions.

You see, the business development process and the way in which we communicate has changed dramatically. Traditional methods no longer produce the results they once garnered.

In the case of this story, just imagine how difficult, or impossible, it would have been to get this executive on the phone to explain our company and services? (*Please know this is coming from us who have built successful businesses over the phone for over a decade!*)

Dialogue through social media cuts through the fog and gets to the point quickly. It is authentic and in real time. From a competitive standpoint, it enables you to reach out and connect directly with people. Of course, you will need to have a compelling reason for that person to respond to you.

Here are some questions to ponder before you can expect the same type of results:

- What are you known for through your on-line presence?

- How many connections do you communicate with on a regular basis?

- Are you sending out a consistent message that others can relate to?

- Are you providing value and resources to your potential connections and market?

- Are you using social media to dialogue with potential clients, or just being a creeper on the sidelines?

If you want some help in setting this up for you and your business, send us a Tweet, or connect on LinkedIn.

58
THE SOCIAL MEDIA DO NOT LIST

Social media has been around now for a few years, and it certainly is not going away. In working with companies, we have noticed an incredible divide happening between those companies embracing this new technology and those who still consider it a waste of time.... aka, *have not done their homework and are looking for a label for what they do not understand.*

For this article we would like to address those business people who are using social media, but are falling into the majority of those who are unaware of the ethics or unwritten rules of this new media. In our workshops and keynotes we have been telling people that traditional media does not apply with social media, yet people are still desperately trying to overlay old methods of advertising with these new models. It just doesn't fit.

Here is our 'Do Not' list that we have accumulated from our work. We hope to catch you before you unknowingly make the same mistakes. Those who have realized they were doing them have all admitted to being boneheads.

- DO NOT spam people with your products and offerings when you have not earned the right. You hate it when it happens to you right?
- DO NOT send the same message out to Facebook, LinkedIn and Twitter. Your mom and old high school buddies are typically not

in business with you.

- DO NOT tell us how wonderful your latest money making scheme is. Network marketing died the first time you bugged your family and friends to buy 100lbs of soap.
- DO NOT beg for 'likes' and bribe us with contests just to get us to follow you. The best way to earn a following is to give them value, not a free iPod.
- DO NOT discuss political or religious beliefs. We see people losing jobs and business because they just can't keep their personal opinions private.
- DO NOT lose the definition and application of DIPLOMACY and RESPECT. If you think everyone agrees with you...give your head a shake!
- DO NOT post anything that someone could not find of value and engaging. Remember people care more about themselves, not how good you are at something.
- DO NOT send game requests to everyone on your contact list. Hey Aunt Mable, I did not know you were involved in the mafia?
- DO NOT slander any other person, no matter how mad or upset you are. Karma can be a real bitch when it comes back to you.
- DO NOT open an account, and not touch it for months. As business relevancy grows, your contribution and ongoing engagement will prove to others you are fresh not rotting away somewhere.
- DO NOT forget the most important part of social media is being social. This means that you're there on a consistent basis and that you engage individuals in conversation – not mass broadcasting
- DO NOT think that just because we connected on social media that I have given you permission to put me on your email list. When I connect with you on social media, I'm giving you permission to do one thing, to talk to me on that social media platform and to START to build a relationship
- DO NOT forget that when you refer someone via social media you are sharing your credibility. This is the one thing you can't afford to tarnish. Be careful whom you retweet or recommend.
- DO NOT forget that your social media presence is an extension and reflection of your brand. What you do on social media builds on the perception people have of you and your company – like it or not.

Ultimately social media is about providing value, ideas and engaging groups of people with similar interests to your own. It is about creating and sharing content in conversations. Of course the best conversations require that you listen more than your speak.   If you catch yourself flogging your lists with your own agenda's, specials and deals of the week.... you will soon find yourself in the long forgotten spam filter.

59
SO YOU WANT TO BETTER UTILIZE LINKEDIN FOR BUSINESS

14 Tips from the Trenches

The growth of social media in business application has undoubtedly been led by the giant LinkedIn. Although this media has been around for a number of years, the majority of business professionals we interact with are still getting their feet wet. They are now jumping into this service and are looking for what it can do for them, and more importantly what type of results they can achieve.

Every day we see hundreds of people getting into this service, connecting with people......and that's where they sit. As we live in an attention deficit society looking for instant gratification, the patience required to build and maximize the network of connections and measure results in LinkedIn is something foreign to most of its users.

So you've built an account, made some connections, reached out to colleagues and even your old boss. So what's next? This is a question we are asked almost daily.

In our ongoing commitment to provide tools and value to our readers and clients we have developed the following thought processes and action steps to help you and your team better utilize LinkedIn as a business development, marketing, branding and networking tool.

1. **The future of your business is your data base:**
   As with any data base of connections LinkedIn is another valuable tool. Instead of questioning the validity of social media as a concept, look at it as the future of your business connections, because that is exactly what it is.

2. **Post value not self-promotion crap:**
   Even though the majority of Facebook posts are self promotional 'deals of the week', LinkedIn is not your arena for selling your products or services....besides no one cares. The best thing to do is provide value and ideas to people who are connected with you. Solve their business issues, provide sound advice and create your own writing style.

3. **It's not about how many connections you have but the value of the conversations:**
   Neil is often criticized by people who believe he is only pumping up his data base by having over 2500 connections on LinkedIn. In fact, he makes it a point to have regular communications with the majority of his connections and giving them value on a consistent basis. You see, Neil believes this to be his network and data base, so he sees the value in each one of his connections. Numbers aside, it is better to have 50 connections you talk with than 500 you have no idea who they are.

4. **Post your own original thoughts not other peoples':**
   LinkedIn is a great resource for you to post your original thoughts, writing and blogs. You can also share good things your colleagues are working on. Avoid passing along other people's work and web site links unless you want people to leave your attention and call your competitor. Your connections need to see you as an original thinker and therefore call you when they want advice or value.

5. **Engage in dialogue, not hide in the weeds:**
   If you are going to take the time to set up your network you might as well say something. We see people everyday standing on the sidelines or hiding in the weeds, taking pot shots at people's contributions. Come on, be bigger than those creep-o-zoids. Get involved in listening, asking great questions and providing more value. (do you see a trend in this providing value thing?)

6. **Don't sign up and then piss off:**
   When developing your profile, please remember to set up notifications to yourself (via your e-mail service) that a new message has arrived. It is always frustrating to reach out to you, send you a message and you don't get back to us for 6 months. If you are only going to check your account every so often, just don't bother setting one up. Part of social media is being responsive and 'in the moment' just like your customers expect you to be.

7. **Ask great questions:**
   You can utilize the 'Answers' section of LinkedIn by both asking great questions and providing feedback to other people's questions. This will keep you engaged with your active connections and may also land you some new ones as well.

8. **Do not send generic requests to connect with people.**
   The lazy person will send the generic connection request, 'Hi, I would like to add you to my professional network'. Of course you would never do that; but we see these in our InBox every day. We have even been guilty of this act in the early days. We now know better. There is something to say about being human and sending people self written requests to connect with some background information. Give it a try.

9. **Freak people out who want to connect with you.**
   When someone sends you 'the generic request', send them back the following response. (remember....be nice) 'Hello (name) thank-you for connecting with me on LinkedIn. I am not certain if we have ever met in person, but I look forward to following your insights and writing on social media and LinkedIn. I will take a look at your profile and web site right away. Please let me know why you wanted to connect and how you want to dialogue together. All the best.' The responses you will receive back will be really cool.

10. **Follow people's lives but don't be creepy:**
    Everyday day you should receive 'status updates' of your connections. These updates from your connections include promotions, new positions and additions to expertise. Be human and send them a note of congratulations or feedback. The responses you get back will be real and could open up new

155

dialogue.

11. **Watch who views your profile, or who is creeping you:**
    On your homepage down the right hand column, you can see who has viewed your profile. This is a great tool to keep an eye on who is checking you out....a potential client, a friend or even your competition. We do not recommend you jump on them right away, just make a mental note to connect with them at a later date.

12. **Keep an eye on (your) the trends:**
    There are tracking tools on Linkedin that let you know how you are doing in search results and views. Use this as a dashboard to ensure your influence is always increasing and improving. If your numbers are flat....you are being too boring.

13. **Remember the days of the recruiter and headhunter?**
    If you are either looking for a start to your career, a change or even looking to hire, the 'Jobs' sections of LinkedIn is now a resource being utilized by most companies we work with. As an employer, an investment of around $400 is all it takes to attract the same quality of candidates as most recruiters can find for you.

14. **What would happen if I Googled you?**
    We have been asking this question a lot in key note situations, and amazed to see all the eyes darting to the floor. Your presence on Google will, in the future, be your credibility in the business world. LinkedIn is very Google search engine friendly and will certainly impact your place in the front page results.

This list has been produced by years of experience, research and hard work. Building your credible data base on LinkedIn is not something that will happen overnight, but if we can at least help you speed up the process we have done our job.

60
THE FIVE QUESTIONS WE GET ASKED MOST ABOUT SOCIAL MEDIA

Through our daily interactions with business owners and entrepreneurs the topic of social media always comes up and we usually get asked questions like:

- Is it really worth it?
- How much time does it take?
- I don't know where to start – what do I do first?
- What kind of results should I expect?
- What's better, Facebook or Twitter?

There are no standard answers to these questions, because our answer will be based on what social media means to you.

If you believe that social media is just another broadcast tool – a way for you to deliver your message to potential customers, then our answer to you regarding all of the questions above is…don't bother.

You see the community of social media is not the place for promotion. That's the job of your website. Social platforms like Twitter, Facebook, LinkedIn and YouTube are designed for sharing, educating, learning and connecting. While promoting is easy – it's not welcome – at least not until you've earned it.

On your website you can control 100% of your message and if someone takes the time to visit your site, they understand that you will have information about you and what you do. Visitors to your site are comfortable with the fact there will be some self-promotion.

Think of social media as digital communities. They are safe places for people to gather to connect with people they already know (LinkedIn and Facebook) or to connect with people they have common interests with (Twitter). We like to go to these places because we can have conversations and interact with people we're interested in.

So we are writing this to ask you to stop using social media to broadcast your business. We're asking you to use it as it was intended. To take the time to connect with individuals not try to advertise to the masses. To take the time to share what you know, what you've learned and to give it away freely without expectations.

The ROI (Return on Investment) of social media is a great and ongoing discussion and debate. We've yet to find two people that can agree on a formula. Our philosophy is that the time you invest into social media is time invested in meeting people. It's time building your brand reputation and it's time establishing yourself as someone people want to be connected with.

All of those are pretty valuable goals for any business owner.

So going forward use your website to talk about you, what you do and how you can help. Use testimonials and product demonstrations and give potential customers tons of reasons to want to do business with you.

Use your time on social media to give. Give your knowledge, your connections, your opinions and your experiences. Share knowledge and you will attract people to you. Once they see you are genuinely interested in them and in engaging with them they will want to know more about you and what you do.

At that point you've earned the right to tell them about what you do because they've given you permission. Before that you're just using social media like you would a radio spot or print ad – you're interrupting people.

So the next time you want to tell all of your Facebook friends about your $0.99 special…STOP IT!

SECTION FIVE: **HIRING**

Have you ever hired someone, were really excited about what they would do for your business, but then just three months later you're wondering what happened?

As a business owner, you realize the importance of finding talent that will play a key role on contributing to your business strategy. Most, if not all of our clients tell us they are looking for entrepreneurial mindsets and high level performers. They are not interested in traditional employee relationships. They want more.....because the business growth or even survival depends on people contributing far beyond status quo.

We realize that the number one business challenge today is finding, keeping and inspiring good people.

We too are business owners, who have fought in the trenches, struggled with cash flow, sat awake at night thinking about culture, staying ahead of marketing and are way too busy to be interviewing and testing new hires. Seeking help requires more than a transactional recruiting experience. You must hire right the first time!

Because we already work with our clients in the areas of strategy, training, marketing and culture we have been asked to develop a system that will ensure they have the right people in the right seats working on the right strategies with the right accountability structure.

We have worked with hundreds of businesses in advertising, screening, interviewing and planning. We wanted to share with you what we've learned along the way.

If even a few of these ideas will help you strengthen and grow your team, we have been successful in our commitment to you. Our goal is to give you actions steps you can apply right away to your business.

61
TAKING THE GUESS WORK OUT OF HIRING
A SIX STEP TOOL

Recently in our recruiting and hiring work we have found ourselves utilizing a concept we developed a number of years ago for our clients. It is called **'Aligned Values and Qualities'**.

In our ongoing commitment to help you find and keep the right people we would like to share with you how this tool works.

Step One – Top candidates

You have made it through the screening process and initial interview stages.

The top three or four candidates have surfaced and you want them to move forward in your process.

Each candidate has visited the office and has met the full team.

Step Two – Develop your top 10 list

Consider the top 10 values and qualities you feel the ideal candidate will need to possess to work closely with JUST YOU and your expectations.

Write out these qualities, ranking them from 1-10 (1 being the most important) on a sheet of paper.

Place the list in a safe place and move to step 3.

Step Three – Involve your key team players

Identify every person on your team who will be working closely with the new person.

Have each team player write out their own top 10 values and qualities list, and instruct them to rank each quality the same way you did.

Remind them to reflect solely on themselves, not what they think is needed for the full team.

Step Four – Bring the lists together

Find an open wall in the office and have each keep player post their list for everyone to see, yours included.

As a team, stand back and observe everyone's lists on the wall.

We have done this with as few as 3 team members and as many as 20 with amazing results.

From everyone's feedback you are to develop a single list with the synergized top 10 values and qualities.

You now have a company grouping that is ready for the next step.

Step Five – Bring the candidates back

Bring back each candidate for the next step of your interview process.

Provide a blank sheet of paper and ask each candidate to articulate what top 10 qualities or values they possess that would make them the best fit for the company.

In some cases you can take your own list and scramble the words and have the candidate re-rank each description on their own.

Once all candidates have completed the assignment, get your team back together and walk through the responses.

You will be amazed how the best candidate will surface to the top.

Note: Some typical qualities we have observed include a mixture of attitude and skill sets. Here are a few:

- honesty
- integrity
- leadership
- influence
- management
- organization
- work ethic
- communications
- attitude
- objective
- energy
- sociability
- team work
- people skills
- creative
- financial
- assertive
- independent

Step Six – Correlate with a solid profiling tool

Combine your effort with a robust on-line profiling or assessment tool.

We prefer Profiles International's web assessments as it has proven to be the most accurate and includes job matching.

 If you follow these 6 steps, you will always ensure you are hiring the right candidate for your company, for your team and for you.

The next time you are hiring, please give this formula a try and let us know how you make out. As always we are here to help you in any way we can. Good luck.

62
SEVEN TIPS TO ENSURE YOU HIRE THE RIGHT PERSON

You only get one shot at screening, interviewing and hiring the right winners in your organization. You want control and the ability to choose the right people.

1. Get your people and culture involved. Look for fit (not compliance) to your team's dynamics and strengths. Look to hire people who will challenge the status quo and contribute to the culture. But first, know your culture and what makes it work.

2. Utilize Social Media and Technology to source good candidates. Gone are the days of relying on headhunters' data bases. LinkedIn and The Job Bank are great resources to use. Most of these are inexpensive or even free.

3. Ask unique and different questions. Typical questions are practiced and anticipated. Mix it up with questions that will not get a rehearsed response.

- What is the best book you have read in the past year?
- What courses have you taken to improve your skills?

4. Know how to read body language and behavioural signals. This may involve some training or bringing in some help. The payoff is well worth it. There are many things being said beside 'words' in an interview. Learn to recognize the shifts and reactions to questions.

5. Allow the team to interact, observe and provide feedback. Bring in the top candidates to spend time interacting with your team. Everyone's feedback will be invaluable and they will feel part of the process too.

6. Utilize a proven on-line profiling tool. Use a web based tool will help you identify thinking style, behavioural traits and interest that you could miss in the interview. Look for one that does job matching as well.

7. Implement a 90 Day Success Plan. This is the most important and often overlooked part of the hiring process. Please ensure new hires succeed by design, through strong coaching and follow up.

63
HOW WILL YOU ATTRACT THE RIGHT PEOPLE
TO YOUR COMPANY?

12 STRATEGIES THAT WILL BE CRITICAL

We were recently on the phone with a colleague from Vancouver. He asked, *"What's going on in Ontario and what are the best companies doing to prepare for the future?"* This was not a new question for us to answer. With all the global changes and new pressures to compete and hold on to market share, the best companies realize that they must practice classic principles and strive for new ideas in a balanced approach.

We are quickly headed towards a significant labour shortage in light of the retiring Baby Boomers. The companies that will survive are the ones that can attract and retain the top talent, and create an environment that fosters innovation and creativity.

We have put together a checklist of what we have observed and supported in our history working with great Ontario companies. This list is what a number of these companies are doing on a regular basis to build an environment that fosters initiative, engagement and growth. We can certainly say that no one company practices all of these principles all of the time, but they do have goals to improve and strive to be better. We suspect it is that drive to constantly raise the bar that really makes them the best.

It is our wish that the following practices will help you and your team build upon results.

❑Everyone Is Involved

- Everyone has a stake in the outcome
- Everyone contributes to ideas and meetings, talk about strengths
- Everyone is engaged and feels like part of the team
- Everyone understands everyone's roles (job shadowing)
- Everyone is able to lead
- Everyone has access to better themselves

❑Creation and Thinking Rooms

- Innovation and design areas, white boards on the wall
- Free thought space away from work areas
- Games and tools to stimulate thinking

❑Physical Wellness and Health Focus

- Gym memberships, even on-site areas
- An outdoor basketball or volleyball court
- Message and spa days
- Regular 15-20 minute afternoon rest periods

❑Intra-preneural Thinking Rules

- Key people think like business owners
- Traditional 'employee paradigms' no longer exist
- Treat people as a 'team' of partners in the business

❑Results Mean More Than Hours Worked

- Flex hours are available
- Project achievement and results count
- Family balance exists

❑Regular Learning and Development Is Expected

- Training is measured through 'return on investment', not through budgets
- On site library. "leaders are readers'
- Leadership lives beyond books and courses, it lives in action and

results
- Everyone learns something new every day and is recorded

(Learn something new every day, or be beaten by someone who does.)

❏Wall Of Fame Area

- Certificates, photos, recognition, years of service awards
- Reward those who have contributed.
- Publically recognize wins and the players involved

❏Ongoing Robust Dialogue and Feedback About Reality

- Performance appraisals are either abolished, or done differently
- The truth rules. Stories, assumptions and agendas are left at the door
- Reward both innovation and mistakes – on the spot
- Learn to truly talk from reality versus assumptions, stories or theories

❏Huddles Of Commitment and Feedback

- Daily group meetings, timed and everyone has an opportunity to contribute
- Replaces traditional meetings
- Follow up and accountability exists
- Take turns leading the huddles

❏Specific Time Blocked Out For Planning and Strategy Work

- Nothing is more important. No urgencies get in the way
- All work is on behalf of the vision and mission
- Vision lives in communications, not the lobby wall
- People talk about what is possible instead of probable
- Know and understand your market and its trends

❏Daily Communications

- Communicate, communicate, communicate
- Understand most people are not trained to communicate effectively

❏See Change As Essential For Growth And Learning, Instead Of A Threat

Do something new Every day that your competition does not

Some of these principles may seem new world and not typical of most work places today. Get the hint?

If you read through this and think, "*We already do these*," you will not lead the market for long. Perhaps you can ask, *'Where can we truly become better in each of these areas?"*

Do you still want to find the best people? You will not. They will find you. Your job as an owner, manager or team member is to create the reputation that will attract the best!

64
ENGAGING THE MILLENNIAL GENERATION
FOR BUSINESS SUCCESS

Top 8 business lessons we have learned:

Talking with our clients, owners and executives, we are being asked to present ideas in dealing with the Millennial generation, also known as Generation 'Y'. Dealing with and managing the expectations, demands, work ethic, and contribution of this new generation is a topic heard often.

A quick definition of a millennial is anyone who was born between 1981 and 2000, and represent the 20-something group now entering the work arena in full force.

The purpose of this is not to describe the millennial generation as good or bad, but instead to share some advice and teaching experience that we have found work in engaging this group in the world of business today.

Here we would like to share 8 key insights to explain our experiences.

1.   **Ensure clear expectations are communicated and understood**

We see a misalignment here everywhere, within all type of companies. When we ask people what they feel is expected of them, it rarely matches what managers/owners are looking for. We tend to not communicate well, so we all need to be better at this. Younger generations are looking for clear direction, mentoring and support. We need to ensure we get this correct, right from the start.

2.   Follow your passion. (Does this still apply?)

We are asking young people to make career decisions earlier than any other generation. With shortened high school tenure and pressure to find direction, most Millennials are very unclear about where they want to work, as well as direction and goals. Let's help them instead of pressuring their decisions.

3.   Resisting technology is futile

Let's face it, the Millennials are wired and connected. They are the Google generation and utilize new technologies in all aspects of their lives. They use social media and texting as a preferred way to communicate. If your business is not set up to handle technology, you will get left behind.

4.   Giving an 'A', a concept used in teaching that translates well into business

For years, Neil has taught a college business course and have utilized a concept called The Practice of Giving an 'A', originally developed by Ben Zander in his book 'The Art of Possibility'. This technique asks students to grant themselves an A-grade for the course by writing a letter dated the last day of the term explaining in detail what they did in the term to earn this extraordinary grade. The test in human nature on this concept is incredible. Each student grades themselves on their performance, already pre-determined. This practice translates beautifully in the business world via the power of individual vision.

5.   Utilize 90 day plans to ensure everyone is on track and focused

This practice is not only critical for the direction and success of your younger employees, but any team member in the organization. Using 3 month planning with measured and reported benchmarks of progress puts the accountability in the owner's court. Your time is spent more in coaching and mentoring, instead of managing and chasing people down. Millennials are looking for independence in most cases.

6.   Please remember the power of recognition

The #1 human need in business is the recognition of a job well done. For the Millennial generation, this is a major factor in job satisfaction. Most managers we work with lack skill and effectiveness in this acumen. Giving proper feedback and praise (when timed and deserved) can be a powerful engagement tool. Please get good at this. Replace yearly performance appraisals with weekly, honest dialogue.

7.   Invite people into your strategy and big picture planning

If you have ever been part of a team photo, the first thing you look for when viewing it is YOU. This is also true for strategic planning. If your team has not contributed to and been part of the development of your business planning process, they can quickly disconnect. Younger generations want and strive for contribution in this fashion; please get them involved.

8.   Please teach financial literacy

Many Millennials have not been exposed to sound financial planning skills such as budgeting, credit, risk and asset/liability knowledge. If you help them create a solid financial, saving and investing mindset, they will commit to your mentorship long term.

This list has been produced by years of experience, research and hard work. We hope these ideas will help you build your winning business team and strengthen your ability to compete and remain relevant in quickly changing markets, demographics and service expectations.

If you are looking for additional ideas to build your team with committed people, working together as a team drop us a call.

65
HANDLING THE REQUEST FOR A RAISE

It amazes us how unprepared most owners are when people approach them and ask for an increase in wage. In many consulting sessions, these scenarios occur time and time again and we have been asked countless times how to prepare for the infamous moment.

"Excuse me but I was wondering if I could approach you for a raise? I have worked here for a while now and feel I deserve more than what I am being paid for. I have worked hard and can promise you that if granted I will work even harder for the company"

This line has been known to strike fear in the minds of most executives. So when this happens to you how do you handle this request?

The following is a set of steps that we have recommended for years, we hope they help you.

Step One: Get up on your desk and dance your face off.

You see, people asking for a raise is not a bad thing. They have developed a level of courage in making a request to be recognized at a higher level. This is an opportunity to celebrate the fact that one of your people desire more for his or her life.

Step Two: Congratulate their courage.

This is a vital step as you want to recognize the courage this person took to approach you in the first place. This is not the time to look weak as a leader. If you handle this wrong you will be dealing with a person who may decide to leave, but stay.

Step Three: Up to this point.

Make it very clear to the individual that, up to this point, they have been compensated as previously agreed to the amount and quality of work they have done. Explain how you appreciate all they have done for the company up to today. The basis of your conversation now is about moving forward, not looking back.

Step Four: Agree with wanting to see them improve.

Explain that you, more than anyone, would like to see this person receive a raise and improve their performance. (Remember raises, improved performance and better results go hand in hand.)

Step Five: Develop a mutual plan to hit stretch goals

Sit with the candidate and have them articulate to you how they want to improve performance that will impact the bottom line of the company. When the employee understands that they will be required to either grow sales, reduce costs or improve efficiencies, the company will then be able to 'afford' the increased compensation.

Note. They are as accountable to the development and execution of this plan as you are, if not more.

Step 6: Make it happen in 90 days

Get them on a clear roadmap to success. They should report back weekly at first, then in 30, 60 and 90 days what they have accomplished. Once performance improvements have been made, measured and sustained then the increase is well warranted.

Step 7: Know how to handle the lazy ones.

For those thinking they deserve the raise based on past performance alone, unwilling to improve, may not be the best people for your culture. They want to hold you hostage to past performance and frankly this is not the best strategy out there. Know how to deal with these people quickly and swiftly. Once you put them on the spot with performance planning and clear expectations they just may come around.

As always if you need help with any of these steps we are just a phone call or email away. We look forward to talking with you.

66
GETTING READY FOR YOUR PERFORMANCE APPRAISALS

Are you getting prepared for your upcoming performance appraisals process? How do you feel? If you are like most, balancing time and workload are on your mind. You want to do a thorough job, but fear this project is a long and intense process. You want to ensure you engage in powerful dialogue and ask the right questions.

Would you like some help in making this process more effective in your organization?

Here are some questions we have developed for our client's teams. We hope they may help you.

- What are you accountable for and what shared performance expectations do you agree to?
- What has been working well for you? Not working well?
- What's missing, that if were in place, would enable you to perform at a new level?
- What are your professional and personal improvement goals? How can we help you exceed those goals?
- As it relates to working here, what is important to you? How do we support this for you? How could we improve?
- Please describe your ideal work environment 3 months from now. How is this different than today?
- What ideas do you have to improve the company's performance, customer service, business development?

- What role do you want to play in executing these ideas?
- How do you want to be held accountable for your improved contribution? How should we be accountable to you?

For your consideration:

- Be careful not to judge based on your beliefs, assumptions or views.
- People should be walking away with an understanding of past performance, shared goals and actions plans to improve both themselves and the company.
- Hold them accountable to what they said they would do. Begin to offer appraisals weekly, if not daily as follow up.

67
THE PAPER LION

Abolishing Traditional Performance Appraisals,
There Is A Better Way

Part One: Let's Agree On The Past....Quickly and Clearly.

Here are some thoughts that may help your Performance Reviews. Most people, including myself, have a problem appraising people on what they have/or have not done in the past.

Many of you may be thinking you already do this component well. We challenge you to read on. In visiting many local organizations, people are still resisting these 'annual rituals' and 'flogging sessions'. In one appraisal session, a gentleman was bold enough to admit: "Listen let's just get to the 'but' and get this over with. I have important work to do!" I consider his boss lucky enough to have the honest dialogue that will allow her to see the need to re-invent this process.

Reviewing past performance is important in its historical context. Something new is to change the context to **what they intend to do in the next # of months and how they will benchmark and appraise themselves for improvement**.

Let's focus on setting the stage for the conversation.

We do need to address the past. Try to mix in 'past based' questions like: *What are at least 3 things you have accomplished this past year that has brought more value to the organization? Please articulate the real value. (Increased production, decrease scrap, increase sales....etc.)*

Get real numbers here, no fluff or lip service. Just the facts please.

If someone gives you a story, ask them for their written notes and specifics. No stories allowed.

What have you done to better yourself personally and professionally in the past year?
What have you learned, on your own accord, in the past year?
How specifically do you use these new skills?
How are these new skills different for you?

Have a robust dialogue about past performance. Look at the relationship from all sides. (Measure yourself as well, and your ownership in this matter.) You can compare rankings in certain areas. Have them rank themselves, you rank them, the team ranks them, heck even including customers, suppliers and vendors may be in order. The essence of this philosophy is to come to an agreement (a real agreement) quickly and move on. Create common ground and a starting point from which all other conversations are based. If this common ground is lacking, all parties will be speaking and listening from different platforms......very dangerous.

Be careful not to use the word 'but' or 'however'.
Here is how it will sound. *"Rick, I met your wife in the mall last night. She is a wonderful person **but**.......ouch!"*

Be careful not to judge people based on 'your views', 'assumptions', 'judgments' etc.... They should be walking away with an understanding of past performance, expectations, goals and action plans to improve both themselves and the future of the company.

In Part Two, we will look at using future benchmarks and coaching in the appraisal process. Creating an environment that allows people to declare what they are going to do differently in the future, versus what they have done in the past.

Part Two: Commit To The Future Together.

In Part One we looked at agreed upon and robust dialogue about past performance.
Now for the next dialogue: based on future goals, plans and benchmarks.
We like to work more on the future planning than on assessment. Let them

assess themselves against their own standards and goals. As a boss, we must be careful to not assess people against the 'world according to you'. Although we know where they need to go, **they MUST articulate it to you, from their mouths**, not ours. By doing this, **they create the ownership of the change or goal**.

From us, it turns into a 'to do list', and quickly looses momentum. Please remember, managers tell people what they should do, while coaches allow people to determine their own destiny and risks for failure. People will choose on their own where they see themselves fitting into the culture and strategy of the company.

Assessing performance based on their ownership is easier for you as a mentor. Now you are simply holding the mirror up to the commitments they made.
What's working?
What's not working?
What's really getting in the way?
What are you now aware of?

How are you showing up on stage, and what are you willing to do about it? These are all good questions to **hold people accountable for what they need to do.** Your influence as a manager is gone. Real accountability is holding up the mirror to people. **They are rewarded by doing the things they (not you) said they were going to do.**

Get them to look at their past performance with you. Compare notes. Have a hearty and robust discussion. Get into a two way dialogue. If the dialogue is leaning 'one way', make sure you are not doing most of the conversing.

Get them into their own plan quickly. Throw in benchmarks. As a coach, ensure they are reaching their benchmarks. Coach by digging down on benchmark options and areas of improvement. They will typically only be aware of a small number of improvement options. Challenge them to create. Ask what else they can do in the matter. The more options the better. Each option is an opportunity for you to coach in the future. Allow them to see improvement as infinite.

Consistently allow them to see where they stand in relationship to their plan and how it correlates with the organizational Strategic Plan.

Never give them answers. They lose power. **Drive them to design their own 'future'.**

Allow them to see the value they bring (or not) to the organization. No excuses, no crybabies, no whiners. You are very strict on this fact. If you hear an excuse (as you know you may) challenge it. Ask them what they intend to do about it to live their plan. Give them the new business reality. Only by being different will their results be different.

Push them to challenge their paradigms, habits and behaviors......every day. This is your #1 job.

The new performance appraisal mechanism: Begin to offer appraisals and feedback weekly, if not daily.

And finally;
HOLD THEM ACCOUNTABLE FOR WHAT THEY SAY THEY ARE GOING TO DO!!!!!
GET THEM INTO ACTION!
NO CRYBABIES ALLOWED!!!
IT'S EITHER EXECUTION, OR EXCUSES!!!

Please remember to call your coach before any conversation. A different perspective can be critical to the success of your initiatives.

SECTION SIX: **CASE STUDIES**

The following section details actual situations from some of our clients.

CASE STUDY ONE:
ACCOUNTABILITY HAPPENS DAILY

Situation

A new promotional products firm was looking to grow business development in the Southern Ontario market.

This niche market has witnessed significant increase in the number of competitors in the past two years and the recession has seen major decline in orders. **The same business model was no longer working.**

This group was very good at attracting young, energetic people to its team, however they lacked experience and sales acumen. The owners felt it was better to hire on attitude and enthusiasm first, and train for skills and acumen later.

They wanted us to help them speed up results.

They also had a sophisticated Client Relationship Management (CRM) system that was ready for use. They also realized the average CRM failure rate was approximately 90%. They did not like the odds.

They knew they needed to be different.

Recommendation

We agreed that to grow the business, short-term training and workshops were not good enough. To harness the potential in each of the sales reps, an ongoing development program, linked to daily accountability was required. Each rep was to see the true value of the measurement criteria and how it was designed to help them succeed. We helped them first engaged their group in a learning culture, and secondly coached them to take ownership of results and achieve targets. Coaching occurred daily, not weekly, monthly or quarterly.

We coached the owners to become coaches, who in turn, coached their team.

Outcome

For the past two years this organization has successfully achieved double-digit sales growth. Each member of the team understands their contribution to the bottom line and accountability is expressed daily. Initiative and follow through is not a management request, it is part of their culture.

They are taking market share when their competitors struggle to cover overhead and meet payroll. This company continues to invest in its people and growth. They have it figured out

CASE STUDY TWO:
LOOK AT YOUR CUSTOMERS FIRST

Situation

A company with an extensive customer database was struggling to retain its customers. They were facing declining sales and losing customers on a monthly basis.

At the same time, they were not getting all of their existing customer's business. Thus leaving dollars on the table.

Recommendation

Customer retention is a key to growth for any company. So the first step was to determine how many customers' they actually had.

Once we had that number, we then segmented the customers based on value and put them into three groups: A's, B's and C's, with A's representing the top 20% of customers.

As a side note, recently as an exercise we've asked a number of key clients to identify their top 20%. Initially they laughed it off and said of course we know who they are, but when the list was actually created, they were shocked and amazed at who was on it.

Recommendation

Once the three groups were identified we then created profiles of each.

This helped to clearly identify their needs and key motivators.

We then took this information and crafted messaging customized for each segment. This made the communications more relevant and focused. The goal was to bring them back in light of increased competitor activity.

Each segment was communicated with over a 90-day period with measurements in place including inquiries, web traffic and sales per customer.

The front line staff was also trained to better engage customers. They learned how to talk less about their products and services and to listen more and give value first.

Outcome

After following a strict 90-day plan, customer attrition stopped and it actually reversed. Also sales per customer increased with "A" and "B" customers

CASE STUDY THREE:
WHEN THE PHONE STOPS RINGING

Situation

A Niagara based welding supply company was experiencing changes in their market. The phone had simply stopped ringing.

For over 10 years the company saw steady growth, but over the last 18 months with the changes to the economy, the phone went silent and this caused a 40% decrease in sales.

The management team looked at their situation and determined that their sales team was not properly prepared for their new reality and that a significant shift was required.

The brutal reality was that the sales team were order takers not business developers. They were great at taking calls and turning them into orders, but when faced with the task of having to go out and find new business they were not prepared.

Add to this that the sales team was spread out across Canada, it added up to a major challenge for their continued success.

Recommendation

The management team thought they needed sales training, but what they really needed was a complete shift in thinking.

Sales training typically produces only short-term results, more like a band-aid solution. We proposed creating a complete revamp of their sales department and sales system.

First we assessed the current skill level of all the sales people and compared them against what the management team felt was an "ideal" sales person. This consisted of an online test and individual meetings to assess the team's abilities.

We then worked with each sales person to develop a 2-page business plan outlining how they were going to grow their accounts over the next 12 months. This is what they would ultimately be held accountable too.

The next step was to address the skills gap with each individual sales rep. Theory will only take you so far, so we engaged in real life role play scenarios. At the same time we helped each rep to share with the team success stories and specific areas of expertise – best practices.

Recommendation

Each session with the team was video recorded and used much like a sports team does, so that each rep could watch themselves in action and improve on language, body language and confidence.

The last step was to work with the sales management team to install a new process to manage the team and measure their progress.

Outcome

The sales team saw an increase in their ability to get appointments with key decision makers.

Each sales person stopped talking about their products and services and started selling value. This decreased price objections and solidified relationships because they were now having business conversations not sales conversations.

Even though the economy was still coming out of the recession, sales cycles reduced by 50% and new sales increase by 40% in just 90 days.

CASE STUDY FOUR:
BUILDING YOUR COMPANY'S VISION

Situation

The owner and senior management team of a progressive company heard of the work that we do in getting a team focused on vision, values and goals. They admitted that the typical way of doing a vision: owners go on a retreat, wordsmithing, sermon on the mount and waiting for change and hoping people would buy in, wasn't going to work.

The business has been successful for a number of decades, yet the owner realized that the engagement of people and innovation was more important today than ever.

He realized that his vision and the vision of his senior managers was useless unless it first came from the middle and front line team.

This company has over 150 employees and reaching each level of employee was not going to be a weekend exercise. The owner and senior managers realized this process would take many months. The owner wanted to do it right the first time, coupled with employee engagement and contribution. The management team also agreed on including customers in the process.

Recommendation

It was agreed that the best way to move forward was to select a small group of proven leaders at every level of the organization. This included estimating/sales, office admin, front line operations and one senior manager.

From us they were not looking for a consulting approach, but instead sound facilitation and accountability. The senior manager in the leadership team would assume the responsibility of designing and recommending the best vision for the company and the owner.

Outcome

To involve every level of the organization the leadership group agreed its first mandate was to interview everyone in the company including the owners. Interview questions were mindfully crafted to enlist commitment to the company, values and ideas for improving service and market growth.

The group agreed the best way to capture this feedback was to interview each person face to face. Although this took more time than the traditional take home survey, the feedback was far more real and honest. The leaders could also engage in questions and much needed dialogue.

After a period of three weeks all of the employee interviews were completed. As a number of questions were based upon a powerful future and growth possibilities, the future direction of the company and improved customer service was established.

In the end, a real organizational vision was developed because it involved and engaged everyone in the company.

The next step was to involve the customers and make a presentation. They agreed the best way to do this was through a client focus meeting.

At the completion of this process the company was successful in doing what most companies only dream of; to develop a clear vision that everyone believes in and commits to. It lives in language, actions and accountability. Everyone knows where the company is headed and the role they play in making the vision a success. They know what is in it for them.

By including their customers in the process they strengthened important relationships and eliminated their competitors.

CASE STUDY FIVE:
FINDING AND KEEPING THE RIGHT PEOPLE

In our ongoing commitment to provide easy to use tools and resources, we have developed the following to help you build your team.

1. Commitment

Interview each person in your company and determine their commitment to the organizations and its future growth.

Ask each person to explain existing customer demands and market expectations (what do they know about your business).

Have robust honest dialogue like you've never had before (you can not build and innovate in business with the same conversations that got you here).

Starting immediately have truthful dialogue about aligned expectations.

Do your people know what you expect of them? How do you know?

Having the same robust dialogue, study overall employee effectiveness.

Understand the difference between profitable and non profitable action (being busy doesn't mean anything).

2. Profiling

Determine if you have the right people in the right positions.

Utilize a profiling effectiveness tool that will align your company's thinking style, behavioural traits and top interests with what you expect.

Establish your ideal candidates and test your teams abilities to that same profile (the results will astound you).

3. Hiring

Using the same profiling techniques begin to bring in and hire the right people that fit your predetermined criteria.

Warning: do not do the interviews yourself; you've been in the business too long.

Ensure your questions and interviewing techniques are different and not the norm. The rules have changed – the same old pre-practiced questions will not give you the best answers.

4. Strategizing

Once you have the right committed team you are now ready to plan the business for new possibilities.

This is not about vague business statements that are hung on the lobby wall, this is about clear goals and action steps that will encompass:

• Changing customer expectations

• Understanding new markets and opportunities

• Internal operational excellence

• Organizational learning and training

• Execution

Your vision, goals and strategy is to be observed in language, actions and results…daily (without this test your strategy dies on the wall, the flip chart paper or in the binder on the shelf).

5. Accountability and follow-up

It is critical to develop weekly, monthly and quarterly accountability structures that include accomplishments, progress and shared learning. The best people to drive accountability are found at all levels of the organization.

Let your leaders lead.

ABOUT THE AUTHORS

The Trigger Strategies Formula

Are you happy with sales and growth? Our experience tells us that most companies are not. After our first conversation with a business owner or manager we usually find out they have trouble getting things done because of one of two things:

1) They are not focused on the right things
2) What they used to do successfully no longer produces the same results

Because of this, they are unsure about what to do next. That's where we come in.

What we do
1. **Analysis**: Assessment of your company's capabilities, your market and your team and their skill sets
2. **Planning**: Develop a measurable plan with accountability
3. **Execution**: Hold everyone accountable to aligned expectations, commitments and urgency

What you can expect
1. Grow your sales profitably
2. Develop your people
3. Help you to own your market by being a specialist

And lastly we put everything into action with dates, commitments, resources and accountability. We measure results and help you drive change. Owners tell us they don't want theories and books, they want results.

Trigger Strategies
Business Consultants: Telling It Like It Is

Neil Thornton, Partner, Trigger Strategies.

Neil brings over 20 years of success in coaching, consulting and training to every talk and client he works with. His uncanny ability to read people and see through what seem like insurmountable situations makes him a highly sought after consultant.

Neil has a unique talent for understanding the psychology behind employee behavior, engagement and corporate culture and vision. He has a unique and direct approach that hits straight to the heart in an honest and direct point.

His talks are entertaining and high energy but also filled with great substance and tremendous learning opportunities for those in attendance. You will never forget a seminar by Neil Thornton.

Larry Anderson, Partner, Trigger Strategies

Solving complex business problems is what Larry is best known for. From declining sales to the need to completely rebrand a business Larry has over 20 years experience in sales, marketing, social media and business development.

With experience in media, advertising agencies and franchising, Larry has developed a successful process for business development that is both measurable and repeatable.

His talks are designed to challenge your thinking and to give you specific tools and resources you can put to work immediately. Larry is described as genuine, honest, direct and insightful and his talks make you want to take immediate action.

Made in the USA
Charleston, SC
02 September 2014